Clinicians' and Educators' Desk Reference on the Licensed Complementary and Alternative Healthcare Professions

Developed by

Academic Consortium for Complementary and Alternative Health Care

Partner Organizations

American Massage Therapy Association—Council of Schools
Association of Accredited Naturopathic Medical Colleges
Association of Chiropractic Colleges
Council of Colleges of Acupuncture and Oriental Medicine
Midwifery Education Accreditation Council

ACCAHC Vision

We envision a healthcare system that is multidisciplinary and enhances competence, mutual respect and collaboration across all complementary, alternative and conventional healthcare disciplines. This system will deliver effective care that is patient centered, focused on health creation and healing, and readily accessible to all populations.

Project Managers and Editors

Elizabeth Goldblatt, PhD, MPA/HA, ACCAHC Chair
Pamela Snider, ND, ACCAHC Founding Executive Director
Sheila Quinn, Consulting Editor
John Weeks, ACCAHC Executive Director

Clinicians' and Educators' Desk Reference on the Licensed Complementary and Alternative Healthcare Professions

©2009, Academic Consortium for Complementary and Alternative Health Care (ACCAHC)
3345 59th Avenue SW
Seattle, Washington 98116
206-932-5799
www.accahc.org

Disclaimer
This publication is intended for use as an educational tool only and should not be used to make clinical decisions concerning patient care. Information is subject to change as educational and regulatory environments evolve. In addition, the role of the partner organizations was to identify authors. These organizations have not endorsed the content of the book, and their participation in selecting the chapter authors was not intended as an endorsement.

ISBN: 978-0-557-13108-2

Contents

Preface

Chiropractic, massage, acupuncture and Oriental medicine, midwifery, and naturopathic medicine were in common use before national surveys documented their sizeable footprint within the US healthcare delivery system.

Four national surveys conducted since 1990 have found that at least a third of US adults routinely use complementary and alternative medical (CAM) therapies to treat their principal medical conditions. All four surveys documented the fact that each year Americans schedule hundreds of millions of office visits to licensed complementary and alternative health care professionals at a cost of tens of billions of dollars, most of which is paid for out-of-pocket. The most recent national survey published by the Centers for Disease Control (NHIS 2007) reported that out-of-pocket expenditures associated with complementary and alternative healthcare practices account for approximately 12% of all out-of-pocket health care expenditures in the United States. The discovery of this "hidden mainstream" of American health care is no longer disputed.

These national surveys have also confirmed that the majority of patients who use complementary and alternative medical therapies generally do not disclose or discuss them with their primary care physicians or subspecialists. This lack of interdisciplinary communication is not in a patient's best interest. Making matters more complicated, it is also known that among individuals who use CAM therapies, the majority tend to use multiple CAM practices as opposed to a single modality to treat their medical problems. Regrettably, many individuals seek combinations of conventional and complementary therapies in a noncoordinated rather than an integrated fashion.

The Institute of Medicine, in its report *Complementary and Alternative Medicine in the United States*, has helped set the stage for future research in this area. The report states:

Studies show that patients frequently do not limit themselves to a single modality of care—they do not see complementary and alternative medicine (CAM) and conventional medicine as being mutually exclusive—and this pattern will probably continue and may even expand as evidence of therapies' effectiveness accumulate. Therefore, it is important to understand how CAM and conventional medical treatments (and providers) interact with each other and to study models of how the two kinds of treatments can be provided in coordinated ways. In that spirit, there is an urgent need for health systems research that focuses on identifying the elements of these integrative medical models, their outcomes and whether these are cost effective when compared to conventional practice.

—Institute of Medicine
Report on Complementary and Alternative Medicine in the US
National Academy of Sciences, 2005

In this era of cost containment and healthcare reform, this recommendation needs to become a priority. In order to design and implement such studies, however, we must first define and describe each of the relevant CAM modalities and professional groups in order to establish standards that lend themselves to reproducible research. Moreover, referrals between professional communities and the training of multidisciplinary teams consisting of both conventional and complementary care practitioners cannot begin unless and until all participating professional groups learn more about one another.

This *Desk Reference on the Licensed Complementary and Alternative Healthcare Professions* contributes enormously to the goal of designing, testing, and refining models of multidisciplinary, comprehensive, integrative care. It thoughtfully yet concisely describes each of the major complementary and alternative health care professions. This information will be very useful to patients, healthcare professionals, educators, students, and those responsible for future clinical research and healthcare policy. The Academic Consortium for Complementary and Alternative Health Care is to be commended for making this information readily available.

There is a Chinese proverb which reads, "The methods used by one will be faulty. The methods used by many will be better."

Over the next decade, let us test this idea, collaboratively and with all the scientific rigor, clinical expertise, and integrity we have to offer. The next generation will surely thank us.

David Eisenberg, MD
Director, Osher Research Center
Division for Research and Education in Complementary and Integrative
    Medical Therapies
Harvard Medical School

August 12, 2009

Foreword

This handbook is arriving on the health care scene in the midst of tumultuous debate about reforms in the US health system. As such, it contributes to the dialogue in a substantive way by providing, logically and clearly, well-organized descriptions of the major complementary healthcare professions.

Three issues received considerable attention in a recent Institute of Medicine Summit on Integrative Medicine and the Health of the Public (February 2009).

- The US has an inadequate primary care workforce. Increasingly, there is recognition that there are licensed CAM practitioners who are prepared to be the first point of entry for many patients. There are also advanced practice nurses who can serve as primary care providers. Current workforce planning needs to take into account a broader range of providers.
- There was also considerable discussion regarding the need to re-orient the system from one that focuses on disease to one that also promotes health. CAM providers have much to contribute in both health promotion and disease treatment.
- Given the complexity of disease and the multiple challenges to human health, rarely can one provider meet all of the physical, emotional, psychological, and spiritual needs of a patient. A team approach that takes into account the capacities of a full range of providers, including CAM practitioners, is critical.

We believe that the time is right for a well-planned and deliberate strategy to integrate licensed CAM practitioners into the nation's healthcare system. These providers are well positioned to focus on prevention, lifestyle change, health promotion and coaching, and management of certain chronic diseases and painful conditions.

This type of integration has the potential to increase quality while decreasing costs of health care.

This handbook offers an orientation for the healthcare teams of the future. Many conventional providers simply do not know enough about the training, scope of practice, and evidence supporting many of the complementary therapies and practitioners described here. This book helps to bridge that information gap.

In the future, we would like to see more practical and detailed descriptions of interdisciplinary team collaborations between physicians, advanced practice nurses, physician assistants, and physical therapists from the conventional medical world and the licensed CAM practitioners listed in this handbook. The processes facilitating referral, interdisciplinary communication, and team building are perhaps the topic of a follow-up handbook that will be essential for the next phase of evolution into true interdisciplinary and transdisciplinary healthcare teams.

As members of the Consortium of Academic Health Centers for Integrative Medicine, our work has involved beginning the process of bringing mainstream medicine, nursing, and allied health professionals into a positive relationship with complementary therapies and disciplines. Much remains to be done in these areas.

However, the benefit of a handbook such as this one is that it creates a common ground in which patient-centered care is central and in which respect for others with professional skills and perspectives different from our own is encouraged. We see this type of publication as a helpful textbook and reference not only to the CAM community but to the conventional health care professions as well.

Victor S. Sierpina, MD, ABFM, ABIHM
Professor, Family and Integrative Medicine
Chair, Consortium of Academic Health Centers for Integrative Medicine
University of Texas Medical Branch
Galveston, Texas

Mary Jo Kreitzer, PhD, RN, FAAN
Director, Center for Spirituality and Healing
Professor of Nursing
University of Minnesota

Adam Perlman, MD, MPH
Executive Director, Institute for Complementary and Alternative Medicine
Vice Chair, Consortium of Academic Health Centers for Integrative Medicine
University of Medicine and Dentistry of New Jersey-School of Health Related Professions

July 2009

Section I

Introduction: An Endpoint and a Beginning

Introduction: An Endpoint and a Beginning

John Weeks and Elizabeth Goldblatt, PhD, MPA/HA

The Institute of Medicine (IOM) of the National Academy of Sciences published *Complementary and Alternative Medicine in the United States* in 2005. The authors described the context of emerging integration behind the IOM exploration and the "overarching rubric" that should guide the integration of these practices with conventional medicine:

> The level of integration of conventional medicine and complementary and alternative medicine (CAM) therapies is growing. That growth generated the need for tools or frameworks to make decisions about which therapies should be provided or recommended, about which CAM providers to whom conventional medical providers might refer patients, and the organizational structure to be used for the delivery of integrated care. The committee believes that the overarching rubric that should be used to guide the development of these tools should be the goal of providing comprehensive care that is safe and effective, that is collaborative and interdisciplinary, and that respects and joins effective interventions from all sources.

> —Institute of Medicine
> *Complementary and Alternative Medicine in the United States*
> National Academy of Sciences, 2005, p. 216

We offer this book in the spirit of the IOM rubric expressed above. This *Clinicians' and Educators' Desk Reference* is meant to be a practical tool for fostering better-informed collaboration and for making clinical practices more safe and effective. This text will help practicing clinicians, academics, and the students who will comprise the next generation of practitioners to become well-informed, mutually respectful team members on whom optimal healthcare delivery rests.

This handbook is also intended for use by well-educated consumers of health care who are frequently building their own teams of clinicians from a variety of health professions. The publication marks the endpoint of a collaborative effort that we envision as supporting an emerging era of inter-professional respect, education, and practice.

The book focuses on the five licensed complementary and alternative healthcare professions, the members of which are providing the lion's share of integration of complementary and alternative medicine (CAM) among community providers, in clinics and hospitals, insurance and healthcare benefit designs, research and educational grants, government programs, and academic centers throughout the United States. The five are chiropractic, naturopathic medicine, acupuncture and Oriental medicine, massage therapy, and direct-entry midwifery. These professions have all achieved an advanced level of regulatory maturity, including attaining the important professional benchmark of earning United States Department of Education (DoE) recognition for the agencies that accredit their educational institutions. These five complementary healthcare disciplines represent roughly 350,000 practitioners nationwide.

In order to support expanded understanding, informed referrals, and choices across the entire integrative practice domain, we also offer information on the related fields of yoga therapy, holistic medicine, holistic nursing, integrative medicine, homeopathy, and Ayurvedic medicine.

Together, the practitioners from the licensed CAM professions and related fields represent the integrative healthcare professionals whom a practitioner is most likely to encounter in developing a more integrated team of community resources for patients. They are also the integrative practice professionals who may also be seeing the patients of many conventional providers, with or without their knowledge.

We hope that this book, in its present form and in future editions, becomes a useful "tool and framework," in the words of the IOM text, not only to "make decisions about …CAM providers to whom conventional medical providers might refer patients," but also to ensure that members of the distinct disciplines whose practices are portrayed here are well informed about each other.

Supporting Multidisciplinary Care: A Focus on Practitioners Rather than Modalities

In this era in which the need for better treatment of chronic disease dominates the healthcare reform dialogue, multidisciplinary teams form the foundation of most of the significant new clinical models. A team approach to health care provides higher patient satisfaction and better health care, and reduces costs. Advocates of the chronic care model, of prospective health care, of the medical home, of integrative medicine, and of functional medicine, all promote an increasingly multidisciplinary medicine. Success in such teams begins with quality information about the skills and background of potential contributors from diverse professions.

Practitioners of all types tend to be educated in silos. We have a saying in the Academic Consortium for Complementary and Alternative Health Care (ACCAHC) that "those who are educated together practice together." If we wish to develop a patient-centered healthcare system, then we must break out of these isolated silos and learn more about one another.

This book is distinguished by its focus on practitioners and their philosophies. Our authors explore approaches to patients, education, accreditation, scopes of practice, and professional developments. We worked with key national educational organizations to select authors whose rich experience as clinicians and educators would inform the writing.

This orientation is in contra-distinction to most education and publications relative to complementary and alternative practices. Past contributions focused mainly on individual agents, modalities, or therapies. Insufficient attention has been given to exploration of the whole systems of care which the distinctly licensed CAM practitioners are educated to provide. Too often, the portraits of these professions, when they are offered, come from outside observers rather than from those with personal experience as practitioners.

The historically limited focus of most texts targeting multidisciplinary audiences does a disservice to both practitioners and consumers. A description of a single natural therapy, for instance, will not teach about the context in which it is offered by an actual practitioner. The reader will not encounter the profession's distinct approach to patients, the depth of the professional education which informs it, and the sometimes surprising scopes of practice that underlie it. Approaches may include conventional and nonconventional diagnostic strategies, together with diverse treatments from their own disciplines.

In addition, a reductive focus on CAM therapies for specific diseases, such as a botanical or the use of acupuncture needles, does not teach a community practitioner that the healthcare disciplines portrayed in this book tend also to emphasize preventive medicine, the practitioner-patient relationship, the promotion of wellness, and the teaching of self-care practices. These disciplines reflect whole systems of care rather than more limited modalities or therapies. The loss of knowledge and skills in using a reductive focus can be significant. An excellent perspective on potential problems is provided by the IOM report on CAM cited above:

> Although some conventional medical practices may seek and achieve a genuine integration with various CAM therapies, the hazard of integration is that certain CAM therapies may be delivered within the context of a conventional medical practice in ways that dissociate CAM modalities from the epistemological framework that guides the tailoring of the CAM practice. If this occurs, the healing process is likely to be less effective or even ineffective, undermining both the CAM therapy and the conventional biomedical practice. This is especially the case when the impact or change intended by the CAM therapy relies on a notion of efficacy that is not readily measurable by current scientific means. (p. 175)

A modality or therapy orientation also falls short in assisting students, educators, and clinicians to understand how to communicate with and work in teams with other practitioners, and renders a disservice to consumers as well. Patients are too often treated by professionals who have neither the knowledge nor comfort to work well with members of these complementary healthcare professions who may, in a given moment, offer just what will serve the patient best. This book, while foundational, is also therefore remedial.

Additional Context for this Book

We have taken a perspective that is part of a broader shift in the integrative practice and CAM dialogue, just as it is part of the heightened focus on multidisciplinary teams in the broader health reform effort.

In 2005, for instance, the Consortium of Academic Health Centers for Integrative Medicine (CAHCIM), consisting now of 45 member institutions, changed its operating definition of integrative medicine. The amended definition emphasizes the importance of integrating not only "modalities" but also "healthcare professionals and disciplines." (See the Definition of Integrative Medicine at http://www.imconsortium.org/about/home.htm.)

The commitment of educators and accreditation officials from the five licensed disciplines featured in this book to form ACCAHC as an independent organization is also evidence of the emerging multidisciplinary universe. While the artifact called "CAM" neatly bundled these distinct disciplines into a group, in truth, these professions also emerged in separate silos. ACCAHC represents the growing recognition of leaders in these fields that their students are increasingly entering an era that values skills in multidisciplinary teams. Membership in ACCAHC reflects a commitment to developing new knowledge, skills, and attitudes.

The research environment also offers evidence of this shift toward broader dialogue from the limited focus on the use of individual agents. In 2008, Josephine Briggs, MD, the director of the National Institutes of Health National Center for Complementary and Alternative Medicine (NCCAM), announced a shift toward effectiveness research and real world outcomes. (Weeks J. Roadmaps for Our Future: An Interview with NCCAM Director Josephine Briggs, MD. Available at http://www.integrativepractitioner.com/article_ektid13196.aspx) Attendees of the 2009 North American Research Conference on Complementary and Integrative Medicine, the most significant research meeting for integrative practice, witnessed a noticeable increase in program content relative to whole systems of care, patient-centered outcomes in care that focus on the whole person, and the challenges in capturing outcomes of actual practices. (See www.cahcimabstracts.com.)

This refocusing of the integration dialogue is also reflected in the call from leading health reform leaders such as US Senator Tom Harkin (D-IA) to orient reform toward creating a "wellness society." Early legislative language from the US Senate includes establishing a new wellness council to guide the nation in this direction. Language supporting inclusion of complementary and alternative practitioners, integrative medicine approaches, and integrated care can be found in various sections of early drafts. This focus on wellness and prevention is aligned with the health orientation and wellness principles of the licensed CAM professions and related integrative practice disciplines.

We believe that the time is ripe for this practical desk reference. We have organized this book to facilitate ready access to useful information. In this section, we begin with some general information on the five licensed complementary healthcare professions. We then share our strategy on the collaborative process through which we developed the book's content, including the template the authors were asked to follow. We close this section by providing more information about the Academic Consortium for Complementary and Alternative Health Care (ACCAHC). This leads directly into the book's second section, a detailed look at some of the collaborative, inter-professional activity with which we continue to be involved. The third section includes the chapters from each of the five licensed complementary healthcare professions, and the Appendices contain similar information on the related integrative practice fields

Data on the Licensed Complementary Healthcare Professions

As noted above, the five licensed complementary healthcare professions have each distinguished themselves by achieving certain benchmarks of professional development. These benchmarks include creating councils of colleges or schools, finding agreement on consistent national educational standards, establishing an accrediting agency, and then earning recognition of the accrediting agency by the US Department of Education. Each achievement marks a stage of maturation.

In addition, each of these licensed professions has also created a national certifying or testing agency, which is important to the public and to state regulators as the profession begins the long process of promoting licensing in each state. To expand licensing, initial groups of practitioners in each state formed state associations, mustered political skills and courage, and created coalitions of supportive patients and consumers to mobilize members of one legislature after another to enact licensing statutes for these professions.

Success in achieving these benchmarks is a prerequisite for integration into the broader healthcare enterprise in the US. Members of these disciplines are able to meet core credentialing standards for participation in conventional payment and delivery systems.

Table 1.1 provides data on the status of each profession in these benchmarking processes. As is clear, while all five disciplines have a federally-recognized accrediting agency, the number of states in which licensing has been established varies significantly.

Table 1.1

**Development of Standards
by the Licensed Complementary and
Alternative Healthcare Professions**

Profession	Accrediting Agency Established	US Department of Education Recognition	Recognized Schools or Programs	Standardized National Exam Created	State Regulation*	Estimated Number of Licensed Practitioners
Acupuncture and Oriental medicine	1982	1990	54	1985	44 states	25,000
Chiropractic	1971	1974	16	1963	50 states	75,000
Massage therapy	1982	2002	97	1994	43 states	250,000
Direct-entry (home birth) Midwifery	1991	2001	11	1994	26 states	1,500
Naturopathic medicine	1978	1987	7	1986	15 states	4,500

*For chiropractors and naturopathic physicians, this category uniformly represents licensing statutes; for acupuncture, virtually all states use licensure; for massage, there is a mixture of licensing, certification, and registration statutes.

Partnerships with National Organizations for Content

Many questions arise when considering a publication to describe a number of disparate professions. How can one most equitably develop a respectful and useful resource? Who should be charged with authoring the chapters? How can we ensure balance and accuracy?

We chose to address these questions by working with and through authors selected by leading national educational organizations affiliated with the five professions. For the core chapters (section III), we contacted the councils of colleges and schools which are organizational members of ACCAHC. For direct-entry midwifery, we worked with that profession's accrediting agency. While these organizations helped us identify authors with whom we worked to completion of the book, the partner organizations did not endorse the content of this section, their chapters, or the book as a whole.

For the appendices, we secured authors who were selected by the leading professional organization in the field. For integrative medicine, which is not a profession per se, we worked with the Consortium of Academic Health Centers for Integrative Medicine. Table 1.2 lists the partners and authors. We are deeply grateful for all their contributions.

Table 1.2

Partner Organizations and Authors

Chapters	Partner Organizations	Authors
Acupuncture and Oriental Medicine	Council of Colleges of Acupuncture and Oriental Medicine	David Sale, JD, LLM Steve Given, DAOM, LAc Catherine Niemiec, JD, LAc Elizabeth Goldblatt, PhD, MPA/HA
Chiropractic	Association of Chiropractic Colleges	Reed Phillips, DC, PhD Michael Wiles, DC, MEd David O'Bryon, JD
Massage Therapy	American Massage Therapy Association Council of Schools	Jan Schwartz Cherie Monterastelli, RN, MS, LMT
Direct-entry Midwifery	Midwifery Education Accreditation Council	Jo Anne Myers-Ciecko, MPH
Naturopathic Medicine	Association of Accredited Naturopathic Medical Colleges	Paul Mittman, ND, EdD Patricia Wolfe, ND Michael Traub, ND, DHANP
Appendices		
Ayurvedic Medicine	National Ayurvedic Medical Association	Felicia Tomasko, RN
Holistic Medicine	American Holistic Medical Association	Hal Blatman, MD Kjersten Gmeiner, MD Donna Nowak, CH, CRT
Holistic Nursing	American Holistic Nurses Association	Carla Mariano, EdD, RN, AHN-BC, FAAIM
Homeopathy	American Medical College of Homeopathy	Todd Rowe, MD
Integrative Medicine	Consortium of Academic Health Centers for Integrative Medicine	Victor Sierpina, MD
Yoga Therapy	International Association of Yoga Therapists	John Kepner, MBA

Note: More information on the authors is provided with each section.

Templates for the Chapters and Appendices

The author or author teams for the core chapters agreed to write approximately 5500 words according to a template that was intended to make this an easy reference guide for readers. For the appendices, we used a similar template, but asked for 1000 words. We gave the authors flexibility in the extent to which each would choose to focus on an individual section from among the following:

Philosophy, Mission, Goals
Characteristics and Data
Clinical Care
     Approach to patient care
     Scope of practice
     Referral practices
     Third-party payers
Integration activities
Education
     Schools and programs
     Curriculum content
     Faculty and other training information
     Accreditation
Regulation and Certification
     Regulatory status
     Examinations and certifications
Research
Challenges and Opportunities
Resources
     Organizations and websites
     Bibliography

The authors understood that their chapters would have to pass muster beyond the borders of their own profession. The content was reviewed by an internal editing team and also by the authors from the other disciplines. If any reviewer felt that another discipline had overstated its value, for instance, the chapter authors were asked to make edits or make their case stronger. Numerous changes were made during this review process.

Collaboration: The Birthing of this Book and the Hope for Its Future

We offer this book as a tool to facilitate greater collaboration and understanding between well-informed practitioners and to support better health care for patients. Respectful collaboration has been our vision and mission since ACCAHC was first conceived. Section II of this book shares advances in cross-disciplinary education and practice over the past half-decade; ACCAHC has been proud to take a lead in developing many of them.

This book also represents collaboration with donors, individuals, and organizations who enhance our ability to fulfill our mission.

We are deeply grateful to Lombard, Illinois-based National University of Health Sciences (NUHS-www.nuhs.edu) for a significant project grant which allowed us to bring this multi-year project to completion. Specifically, we thank James Winterstein, DC, president of NUHS for his support for this grant. NUHS has programs in four of the licensed professions discussed here: chiropractic medicine, acupuncture and Oriental medicine, naturopathic medicine, and massage therapy. ACCAHC also thanks the Council of Colleges of Acupuncture and Oriental Medicine (www.ccaom.org) for a 2007 contribution that supported initial work on this project.

Critical financial support which nurtured ACCAHC through this gestational process has come from Lucy Gonda, who is effectively an ACCAHC co-founder. Her vision and philanthropic support gave us our first boost into life in 2003. She continues to provide key support for our mission. Joining Gonda in the ACCAHC Sustaining Donors Group which supported relationship development and staff time for this book are the Leo S. Guthman Fund, NCMIC Foundation, and Bastyr University. We thank, in particular, Lynne Rosenthal, Lou Sportelli, DC and Daniel Church, PhD, respectively, for their decisions to move these three organizations to back this work.

Finally, this book is a first edition. We anticipate that our collaborators from the councils of colleges and schools and the professional organizations will have ideas about how to enhance their chapters once they see the book in print. We also anticipate developing related curricular and presentation tools for those interested in making presentations based on this content. These will be available through www.accahc.org. We would like to hear from any of you about how we can make it more useful. Ideas can be sent to info@accahc.org.

The publication of this book marks the beginning of a new era of inter-professional respect and practice. Thank you each for your own commitment to expanding your educational or clinical horizon to better understand and respect members of these disciplines. Patients will thank us all for it.

About ACCAHC (www.accahc.org)

[We] envision a health care system that is multidisciplinary and enhances competence, mutual respect and collaboration across all complementary, alternative and conventional health care disciplines. This system will deliver effective care that is patient centered, focused on health creation and healing, and readily accessible to all populations.

—Vision Statement, Academic Consortium for
Complementary and Alternative
Health Care (ACCAHC)

The idea of an organization like ACCAHC initially originated in a series of meetings beginning in the late 1990s: the Integrative Medicine Industry Leadership Summits. Additional impetus was provided by the National Policy Dialogue to Advance Integrated Health Care (2001). In each instance, leading educators in integrative practice recognized the value of creating a vehicle for ongoing interdisciplinary dialogue and action.

These seeds began to take formal shape in 2003 as a project of the Integrated Healthcare Policy Consortium (www.ihpc.info), chaired by Sheila Quinn. The project evolved until the end of 2006 under the direction of Pamela Snider, ND (founding Executive Director) and Reed Phillips, DC, PhD (founding Chair).

ACCAHC's key purpose was to bring educator leaders of the licensed complementary and alternative healthcare professions into one room so they could jointly articulate their shared issues and concerns about the evolving integrative medicine dialogue. ACCAHC allowed educators to create one voice as they joined with their academic counterparts in conventional medicine in the 2005 National Education Dialogue to Advance Integrated Health Care: *Creating Common Ground* (NED), which was led (under IHPC's auspices) by

John Weeks, Snider's successor as ACCAHC executive director. The section of this book titled "Toward Collaboration between the Professions" describes more about the role of NED and ACCAHC in that process.

Once convened in the same room, however, ACCAHC's educator leaders realized there were many additional values in ongoing dialogue and collaboration. These educator leaders determined in mid-2006 that ACCAHC should seek to become an independent entity to imbed this movement as a continuing part of the landscape. ACCAHC was subsequently incorporated as a nonprofit corporation, later obtaining Internal Revenue Service recognition as a tax-exempt 501(c)(3) organization. Table 1.3 lists the organizational members of ACCAHC, each of which pays dues based on the size of the organization.

ACCAHC's core members are those councils of colleges and schools, US Department of Education-recognized accrediting agencies, and nationally recognized certification and testing organizations from the licensed complementary and alternative healthcare disciplines that choose to join. Current ACCAHC membership includes the majority of these organizations. In addition, some accredited schools have chosen to join ACCAHC as individual college members.

As we developed our structure, we also decided not to close the door on professions that are committed to greater self-regulation but have not yet met the benchmarks of the licensed disciplines. Concerns were voiced that, without such a membership provision, ACCAHC would recapitulate the pattern of exclusion that has challenged the maturation processes of the currently licensed professions. ACCAHC developed distinct membership categories for two new groups, traditional world medicines (TWM) and emerging professions. To date, three TWM organizations have chosen to join, as indicated in Table 1.3.

As mentioned above, ACCAHC reflects collaboration with a growing list of donors. Membership funds roughly a third of basic operations with the remainder of operational funding and all major projects dependent on foundation, corporate, and individual philanthropy. We also plan to create additional funding through publication of resources such as this book. Donors not already mentioned who have assisted ACCAHC significantly in advancing our mission include Andrew Weil, MD, Standard Process, Inc., Northwestern Health Sciences University, and the Consortium of

Table 1.3

ACCAHC Organizational Members as of May 2009

Member Type	Member Organizations
Councils of Colleges and Schools	Council of Colleges of Acupuncture and Oriental Medicine www.ccaom.org Association of Chiropractic Colleges www.chirocolleges.org American Massage Therapy Association-Council of Schools www.amtamassage.org/schools.html Association of Accredited Naturopathic Medical Colleges www.aanmc.org
Accrediting Agencies	Commission on Massage Therapy Accreditation www.comta.org Council on Chiropractic Education www.cce-usa.org Council on Naturopathic Medical Education www.cnme.org Midwifery Education Accreditation Council www.meacschools.org
Testing and Certification Organizations	National Board of Chiropractic Examiners www.nbce.org National Certification Board for Therapeutic Massage and Bodywork www.ncbtmb.org National Certification Commission for Acupuncture and Oriental Medicine www.nccaom.org North American Board of Naturopathic Examiners www.nabne.org
Traditional World Medicines and Emerging Professions*	International Association of Yoga Therapists www.iayt.org National Ayurvedic Medical Association www.ayurveda-nama.org Yoga Alliance www.yogaalliance.org
Individual Colleges or Schools	American College of Traditional Chinese Medicine www.actcm.edu Bastyr University www.bastyr.edu Cayce/Reilly School of Massotherapy www.edgarcayce.org/health/crsm_index.html Five Branches University www.fivebranches.edu National College of Natural Medicine/Helfgott Research Institute www.ncnm.edu National University of Health Sciences www.nuhs.edu New York Chiropractic College www.nycc.edu Northwestern Health Sciences University www.nwhealth.edu Western States Chiropractic College www.wschiro.edu

*The Traditional World Medicine category of organizational member was created to allow participation of professions engaged in the educational and professional regulatory efforts described earlier.

Academic Health Centers for Integrative Medicine. The Institute for Alternative Futures provided us with significant in-kind support. Finally, ACCAHC is deeply grateful for the visionary leaders of the Integrated Healthcare Policy Consortium out of whose multidisciplinary, collaborative work ACCAHC was born and then nurtured in its first years.

ACCAHC's projects are led through the Board of Directors and three working groups, one each in the areas of research, education, and clinical care. The projects are diverse, and each includes a focus on supporting inter-professional education, research, and clinical practice. Among current or recent projects are: creating forums to foster exchange on multidisciplinary aspects of patient-centered care between the leaders of ACCAHC member organizations; linking student leaders across the disciplines; development of additional educational materials on the disciplines; developing didactic and clinical training materials to enhance competencies of members of ACCAHC disciplines for practice in integrative settings; supporting ACCAHC institutions in developing inter-institutional collaboration; supporting the development of a stronger research ethos in ACCAHC's educational institutions; developing focused research projects and reporting and publishing them for our peers; and developing materials for educators and young researchers on outcomes, effectiveness, and whole systems research.

Of particular interest recently was ACCAHC's work to support consumer interest in distinctly licensed practitioners during planning and execution of the Institute of Medicine's February 25–27, 2009 National Summit on Integrative Medicine and the Health of the Public. A series of conversations between leaders of ACCAHC and representatives of the IOM led to the appointment of ACCAHC chair Elizabeth Goldblatt, PhD, MPA/HA to the IOM's planning committee. Goldblatt's service included helping form valuable links between the conventionally trained practitioners and educators who were her colleagues on the committee and key professionals in the licensed complementary healthcare disciplines. The rich resources created through the Summit are available through the IOM's site http://www.iom.edu/?ID=52555.

Up-to-date information on ACCAHC's directions and key personnel are on the ACCAHC website at www.accahc.org. We welcome your queries through info@accahc.org.

Section II

Toward Collaboration between the Disciplines: An ACCAHC Perspective

Toward Collaboration between the Disciplines: An ACCAHC Perspective

This chapter was adapted from content ACCAHC made available for a textbook entitled *Collaboration across the Disciplines in Health Care* (Brenda Freshman, PhD and others; Jones & Bartlett, 2009), which ran as a chapter titled "Complementary, Alternative and Integrative Health Care Perspectives." The chapter was co-authored by members of the ACCAHC executive committee at that time: John Weeks, Elizabeth Goldblatt, PhD, MPA/HA, Reed Phillips, DC, PhD, Pamela Snider, ND, Jan Schwartz, CMT, David O'Bryon, JD, Marcia Prenguber, ND, and Donna Feeley, MPH, RN, CMT.

Overview

This book is offered as an educational tool about the licensed complementary healthcare professions and related disciplines. Yet our purpose is more fundamental. Our goal is to create a basis for better understanding and mutual respect between members of distinct healthcare disciplines so that the health care patients receive will be enhanced. Collaboration is the primary tool through which we will achieve that goal.

This chapter explores collaborative activity between educators in conventional academic medicine and educators from the disciplines represented in this text, particularly the five disciplines with federally-recognized accrediting agencies. These are acupuncture and Oriental medicine (AOM), chiropractic, naturopathic medicine, direct-entry (home-birth) midwifery, and massage therapy.

For these disciplines, significant local and national dialogue with conventional medical educators, and among themselves, emerged formally with the turn of the 21st century. We begin with a description of some of the historical context for this activity, including recommendations from the White House Commission on Complementary and Alternative Health Care Policy (WHC, 2002), the Institute of Medicine (IOM, 2005), and the multi-stakeholder and multidisciplinary National Policy Dialogue of the Integrated Healthcare Policy Consortium (IHPC, 2002).

We then focus on the actions and directions set by the collaborative National Education Dialogue (NED) to Advance Integrated Health Care: *Creating Common Ground* (Weeks et al., 2005) and the Academic Consortium for Complementary and Alternative Health Care (ACCAHC). We also note some cross-disciplinary educational initiatives of some members of the Consortium of Academic Health Centers for Integrative Medicine (CAHCIM), a group of 45 conventional medical institutions active in the integrative medicine field (www.imconsortium.org). The chapter includes several sidebars that shed useful light on the activities of some of these entities, and identifies priorities for action collaboratively established by these mixed groups of academics.

Finally, we have included some clarifying values, recommendations, and challenges encountered on this mission to improve health care.

Dynamics Shaping the Emerging Interest in Collaboration

As noted in the Introduction, the period from 1980 to the present has been one of significant expansion for schools, accreditation, licensing, and self-regulatory efforts among the licensed complementary healthcare professions. Communication and collaboration between the complementary and alternative healthcare disciplines and conventional medical professionals have expanded over these decades, yet effective, widespread engagement still lies ahead of us. A long history of exclusion and antagonism separated biomedicine from disciplines promoting holistic, integrative, and natural healthcare practices. While waning, attitudes developed during that period still influence the dialogue. Residual misunderstandings, mistrust, and often ignorance originating during that period of extreme polarization can still shadow efforts to create greater collaboration.

Table 2.1 offers a view of how that history of exclusion created attitudes and perceptions that can still affect interdisciplinary relationships. The bottom line of the table, as with past interdisciplinary experiences, is that both conventional and complementary providers typically saw patients who were the failures of their counterparts on the other side of the divide. Images of the other disciplines were therefore formed accordingly.

Table 2.1

Bilateral Prejudice as an Operational Issue Limiting the Integration of Complementary and Conventional Health Care

Phenomenon	Conventional Perspective	Complementary Perspective
Successful complementary treatment	placebo for self-limiting condition	proof of value of complementary care
Successful conventional treatment	proof of value of conventional care	suppresses problems / fails to address causes
Science in conventional medicine	our foundation	80–90% of procedures have no support for clinical efficacy
Science in complementary medicine	virtually non-existent	strong in some areas / growing body of evidence
Conventional primary care formulary	good tools	70% of problems go away on their own
Complementary primary care formulary	70% of problems go away on their own	good tools
Complementary diagnostics	of great concern / likely to misdiagnose	consider more than lab values
Conventional therapeutics	best in the world	often inappropriately invasive / likely to miss causes
Surgeon quick to operate	overutilizer	rip off artist
Chiropractor always requesting 20 visits	rip off artist	overutilizer
Antibiotics for viral conditions	basically harmless treatment demanded by patients	harmful to the individual and the population
Complementary therapies in end-stage terminal conditions	waste of money/creates false hope	alleviate side-effects of conventional treatment/ help patients with transition
Oncologist creating new chemotherapeutic "cocktails"	brilliant clinician	experimenting with poison
Naturopath who mixes Asian and homeopathic treatments	totally wacko	brilliant clinician
Self-healing	self-limiting condition, spontaneous remission	healing power of nature
Clients of the "other" who come to my office	their failures	their failures

Note: The table was created by John Weeks in 1996 from data acquired from surveys and interviews. While it does reflect early perceptions that framed the integration dialogue, the choice of language does not reflect ACCAHC's current values and approaches. In addition, the phrases used in the table did not reflect the judgments of all providers from either group; they were generalizations.

Source: Operational Issues in Incorporating Complementary and Alternative Therapies and Providers in Benefit Plans and Managed Care Organizations. Prepared for the Workshop, Complementary and Alternative Medicine: Issues Impacting Coverage Decisions, sponsored by the US National Institutes of Health, Office of Alternative Medicine, US Agency for Health Care Policy and Research, and the Arizona Prevention Center at the University of Arizona Health Sciences Center; October 9, 1996; page 45. © John Weeks. Reprinted with permission.

Opening through force: An antitrust lawsuit

In 1990, the chiropractic profession concluded a 15-year antitrust battle against the American Medical Association (AMA), *Wilk vs. the AMA*. The chiropractors' grassroots campaign led to a determination that the AMA had engaged in illegal restraint of trade through such practices as excluding chiropractors from hospitals and forbidding AMA members from sharing patients with chiropractors. Ending the era in which the AMA branded not just chiropractors but all non-conventional practitioners as quacks or frauds created a potential for better-informed dialogue between conventional medicine and all of the alternative and holistic fields.

Understandably, the attitudes and feelings engendered by discriminatory actions are still present today. Physicians educated in the earlier era are now in leadership positions in academic health centers and hospitals. Similarly, many leaders in the complementary and alternative healthcare professions entered their training in a highly adversarial atmosphere. While both conventional and complementary health professionals from that earlier time are embracing the integration process, younger practitioners are typically more influenced by recent cultural trends and are more likely to have personally used complementary approaches in their own care or for that of family members.

Public interest and demand

An extremely powerful force generating early momentum toward improving the flow of information and communication was the evidence that over a third of consumers in 1991 used some form of unconventional medicine and most chose not to tell their conventional providers about it (Eisenberg et al., 1993). Originally reported in the *New England Journal of Medicine* in January 1993, then updated for the *Journal of the American Medical Association* in 1998 (Eisenberg et al., 1998), the survey findings stimulated a fundamental shift in perception among public officials, politicians, and members of the media. Alternative medicine users, it turned out, were everywhere.

Hospitals, academics, insurers, politicians, and employers began exploring how to take advantage of this pervasive consumer interest. Subsequent national surveys have suggested that between 35% and 65% of healthcare consumers currently use some form of CAM. Other surveys have found that individuals with chronic conditions are more likely to explore nonconventional options. The level of consumer use and estimates of cash payments for these services piqued the interest of conventional stakeholders.

Introduction of significant research and education grants

In 1991, via a $2 million Congressional earmark sponsored by Senator Tom Harkin, the NIH was urged to begin exploring what was then termed unconventional medicine. This initiative became the NIH Office of Alternative Medicine, which became the National Center for Complementary and Alternative Medicine (NCCAM) in 1998. The nation's academic health centers, which had heretofore shown little interest in these fields, saw that federal money was a significant new factor in what had originated primarily as a consumer-led movement. New grant funding also supported the interests of conventional academics who saw value in researching nonconventional practices.

NCCAM's annual budget was roughly $120 million in 2008, most of which was distributed as grants to conventional medical centers. Over a dozen significant grants have gone to conventional academic health centers for education-related projects, most to members of the Consortium of Academic Health Centers for Integrative Medicine. Some of these conventional medical schools have had licensed complementary healthcare educator-researchers as advisers; some had AOM or chiropractic or massage or naturopathic institutions as partners. In many of these grants, NCCAM required applicants to have partnerships with complementary and alternative healthcare institutions. Likewise, NCCAM subsequently awarded a series of grants to complementary healthcare academic institutions, with a requirement that they have conventional partners. Most of the current best practices in inter-institutional, collaborative action were initiated through these NCCAM grants.

In short, a major influence for stimulating collaboration was the infusion of federal money from NCCAM, which had been foisted on the NIH by Congressional action. Though some conventional academic leaders were empowered by this opportunity to advance their personal interests or the interests of their patients in complementary and alternative therapies and practitioners, institutional motivation for collaboration was often financial, rather than a more substantive interest in integrating education and/or care.

Emergence of integrative medicine in conventional academic health centers

Closely associated with the availability of research funding was the development of the concept of, and expansion of interest in, what is now called integrative medicine. In 1991, just one conventional medical school was known to have any education relative to complementary and alternative medicine. By 1998, that number had reached 75. The Rosenthal Center for Complementary and Alternative Medicine compiled an extensive list of conventional schools offering course work in CAM, and made the following comment on its website: "At the time we archived the resource (June 2007) it is rare that any conventional medical school would not have courses in complementary, alternative, or integrative medicine."

In 2001, the Consortium of Academic Health Centers for Integrative Medicine (CAHCIM) was formed by nine academic health centers (www.imconsortium.org). To join, a center needed to have institutional support at the dean's level or above, and integrative medicine activity in at least two of the three core areas of healthcare academics (education, research, clinical services). By 2009, the number of CAHCIM members throughout North America had grown to 45. An organization of philanthropists, the Bravewell Collaborative, provided significant backing for the emerging consortium. The development of CAHCIM created a new focal point for collaborative academic activity and shifted the landscape in alternative medicine integration.

Each of these factors opened doors for change agents, inside and outside of mainstream medicine, who believed that health care could be improved through fostering collaboration between conventional professionals and members of disciplines that had historically been ostracized. Most of these professionals were integratively-oriented medical doctors, nurses, or administrators, some of them cross-trained in a complementary and alternative healthcare discipline or modality. Evidence of consumer use allowed these individuals to more publicly promote dialogue, integration, and collaboration.

Yet the ongoing work of these collaboratively-minded professionals, and their partners in the complementary and alternative healthcare disciplines, remains limited by weak institutional support and by the bureaucratic challenges of making change. Optimally, integrative action would be advanced by a desire to understand why patients are drawn to these services, and how care outcomes could be bettered, and/or medical costs reduced, by understanding and integrating these heretofore excluded practitioners. However, the on-going institutional commitments needed to support significant educational, economic, and cross-cultural integration initiatives have often been minimal, making progress very slow.

Promptings from a White House Commission, the Institute of Medicine, and a Policy Initiative

Beginning in 2001, three significant national initiatives provided intellectual and policy-related support for those who chose to begin promoting more exploration of interdisciplinary activity between conventional and complementary and alternative healthcare professions. The report of the White House Commission on Complementary and Alternative Medicine Policy (NIH, 2002) urged that:

> ...agencies should convene conferences of the leaders of CAM, conventional health, public health, evolving health professions, and the public; of educational institutions; and of appropriate organizations to facilitate the establishment of CAM education and training guidelines. Subsequently, the guidelines should be made available to the states and professions for their consideration. (NIH, p. 99)

The Commission endorsed ten guiding principles. One recognizes that "partnerships are essential to integrated health care" (NIH, p. xxiii). Cross-disciplinary understanding and respect are underscored: "Good health care requires teamwork among patients, healthcare practitioners (conventional and CAM) and researchers committed to creating optimal healing environments and to respecting the diversity of all health care traditions."

The 2001 National Policy Dialogue to Advance Integrated Care: *Finding Common Ground* (convened at Georgetown University through the active support of Aviad Haramati, PhD) also published its findings in 2002 and made similar recommendations. This multidisciplinary and multi-stakeholder gathering of 60 leaders in integrated care reached consensus on a core recommendation to "Establish a national consortium of conventional and CAM educators and practitioners." Such a consortium would:

> ... identify a core education for all conventional and CAM educational institutions, created by educators from the respective institutions themselves to ensure that the healthcare professionals of

the future understand what all systems of health care can offer. This will result in healthcare providers, both conventional and CAM, learning at an early point in their training what other systems and modalities offer. The consortium will develop educational standards to ensure that factual and accurate information is taught across all disciplines and that the type of information is in accordance with the teachings and principles of the respective disciplines. (Quinn and Traub, p.12)

The policy-oriented gathering identified a possible need for a special accrediting entity for continuing education and ongoing governmental support for collaborative education:

An interdisciplinary body will be created to accredit continuing education programs in CAM/IHC for all medical disciplines so that medical, nursing, pharmacy students and other health professions students and practitioners, whether conventional or CAM, continue to learn about and respect the value of CAM and integrative healthcare approaches. Federal support is necessary to fund training opportunities in integrative healthcare settings so that medical students and healthcare practitioners, whether conventional or CAM, can learn about integrative approaches in order to provide better and more cost-effective patient care. (Quinn and Traub, pp. 11-12)

Finally, in 2005, the Institute of Medicine published a *Report on Complementary and Alternative Medicine in the United States*, which acknowledged both the growth of the field and the central importance of collaborative and interdisciplinary action:

The level of integration of conventional and CAM therapies is growing. That growth generates the need for tools or frameworks to make decisions about which therapies should be provided or recommended, about which CAM providers to whom conventional medical providers might refer patients, and the organizational structure to be used for the delivery of integrated care. The committee believes that the overarching rubric that should be used to guide the development of these tools should be the goal of providing comprehensive care that is safe and effective, that is collaborative and interdisciplinary, and that respects and joins effective interventions from all sources. (IOM, p. 216)

The report speaks directly to the problems that may arise if integrative medicine confines itself to the best uses of distinct approaches and therapies instead of honoring a medical pluralism that respects significant differences in "epistemological framework(s)" of practitioners from different disciplines.

> Yet, care must be taken not to assume compatibility where none exists. Medical pluralism should be distinguished from the cooptation of CAM therapies by conventional medical practices. (Kaptchuk and Eisenberg, 2001)

> Although some conventional medical practices may seek and achieve a genuine integration with various CAM therapies, the hazard of integration is that certain CAM therapies may be delivered within the context of a conventional medical practice in ways that dissociate CAM modalities from the epistemological framework that guides the tailoring of the CAM practice. If this occurs, the healing process is likely to be less effective or even ineffective, undermining both the CAM therapy and the conventional biomedical practice. This is especially the case when the impact or change intended by the CAM therapy relies on a notion of efficacy that is not readily measurable by current scientific means. (IOM, p. 175)

It is noteworthy that, while this comment urges respect for distinctions between the disciplines, the report itself focused significantly more on integration of therapies than on integration of disciplines. A search by medical journalist Elaine Zablocki found that, in the IOM report, "CAM therapies" appears 299 times, "CAM practitioners" 66 times, "CAM professions" is used eight times, and "CAM disciplines" is used twice. The internal dialogue that was framed was one of grafting truncated therapies rather than the integration of disciplines, with all of their distinct differences and cultures.

While the decisions of many consumers of medicine have already provided ample reason for members of our diverse disciplines to learn to interact more closely, these three national initiatives added necessary perspectives on policy and medical leadership.

Initial Conventional Explorations in Collaborative Education

Between 2000 and 2005, 14 conventional medical and nursing schools and one family medicine residency program received multi-year grants from the NIH NCCAM as part of the Complementary and Alternative Education Project. The October 2007 issue of *Academic Medicine* (Vol. 82, No. 10) devoted 50 pages to nine reports based on these experiences. Of particular relevance to ACCAHC and educators in complementary and alternative healthcare institutions is an article by Anne Nedrow, MD and others about the four academic health centers that formed collaborative partnerships with nearby academic institutions that train CAM practitioners (Nedrow et al., 2007).

Developers of these collaborative programs note that respect for the potential value of complementary and alternative healthcare practitioners is enhanced by giving conventional practitioners direct experience of these approaches in educational, clinical, and research settings. Medical students at Georgetown University, for instance, report surprise in learning, during shared gross anatomy lab, the high level of understanding of anatomy that massage therapists are required to achieve (Weeks, 2006). Confidence of medical students in working with complementary healthcare practitioners increased significantly with personal experience of the therapies among a group of medical students at the University of Minnesota (Weeks, 2006).

Nedrow's integrative medicine program at the Oregon Health and Science University forged ties with Western States Chiropractic College, National College of Natural Medicine (where the dominant program is naturopathic medicine), and Oregon College of Oriental Medicine to form the Oregon Collaborative for Integrative Medicine (www.o-cim.org). Nedrow's conscious effort to put all of the participants in a non-hierarchical relationship, dubbed "lateral integration," was well-received by the complementary healthcare educators. Nedrow has reported that barriers between professionals of different disciplines can be diminished when it is educators who are seeking to collaborate. The shared mission of educators to optimize the education of their students becomes the basis for open-minded collaboration.

Nedrow and her co-authors anticipate that such collaborations will increase. A key emerging issue they identified is credentialing of complementary healthcare practitioners to teach within conventional health professions institutions. The authors recognize that collaboration involves development of respect even in a context of significant differences. One proposed solution is to teach complementary health care "as an aspect of cultural sensitivity."

One sign of emerging openness to collaboration with members of other disciplines is that, by 2007, schools belonging to CAHCIM (for which Nedrow and her co-authors have been leaders) included faculty members who are also licensed members of the chiropractic, acupuncture and Oriental medicine (AOM), and naturopathic medical professions. These educators are presently serving on CAHCIM working groups and participating in their annual conferences. Beginning in 2009, three of these licensed complementary healthcare professionals will serve CAHCIM as co-chairs of their working groups.

An important sign of the emerging spirit of collaboration was a half day of meetings, reception, and dinner involving 95 leaders of CAHCIM and ACCAHC, split roughly evenly, in May 2009. Members of the research, education, and clinical care working groups from the two consortia met to explore shared projects, as did members of the two executive committees. Formal collaborative action is expected to grow in coming years.

Engaging a National, Multidisciplinary Collaboration

In 2004, amidst this rapidly developing environment, the National Education Dialogue to Advance Integrated Health Care: *Creating Common Ground* (NED) was engaged by the Integrated Healthcare Policy Consortium, which birthed ACCAHC. By design, many of the leaders of CAHCIM, as well as the founders of ACCAHC, were involved in the 25-member planning team. NED ultimately included educators from 13 disciplines at a four-day meeting of 75 educators in mid-2005 (see Table 2.2). A parallel process involved the creation of ACCAHC during the same time period (described in Section I).

The 15 months of NED planning revolved around identification and development of a series of projects designed to provide content for the onsite meeting to consider. One project was a survey of all of CAHCIM's integrative medicine programs (then 28) and all of the accredited schools and programs from the ACCAHC disciplines (then 130) to gain baseline data on the "Status of Inter-Institutional Relationships between CAM Disciplines and Conventional Integrative Medicine Programs." Sample findings:

- Few of the then-28 CAHCIM member programs had formal classroom or clinical relationships with any complementary

Table 2.2

Disciplines of Educator Participants in the National Education Dialogue

Acupuncture and Oriental medicine*	Midwifery (direct-entry)*
Chiropractic*	Naturopathic medicine*
Holistic medicine	Nutrition/dietetics
Holistic nursing	Occupational medicine
Homeopathic medicine	Osteopathic medicine
Integrative medicine	Public health
Massage therapy*	Yoga therapy**

*ACCAHC core disciplines.

**Yoga therapy, while not a licensed practice, is involved in ACCAHC as an emerging, Traditional World Medicine discipline.

and alternative healthcare schools or colleges. The greatest involvement was found with AOM schools (32% for classroom, 16% clinical) and massage schools (20% classroom, 20% clinical).

- Belief that developing "stronger, multi-dimensional, interdisciplinary relationships" is key to creating a "fully integrated healthcare system" was strong; 85% of CAHCIM respondents and 86% of the ACCAHC respondents agreed.
- Sharing documents and strategies on best practices was viewed as the most beneficial strategy to support more inter-institutional relationships (73% of CAHCIM and 77% of ACCAHC).

In addition, a set of survey questions directed only at ACCAHC programs found that a majority of respondents had diverse clinical care relationships with conventional delivery organizations in their communities. Among these were community clinics (48%), hospitals (28%), senior homes (43%), and homeless clinics (33%). Such participation was highest in the naturopathic medical field, followed by chiropractic and AOM. The data suggested that integrated clinical services might take place in these off-campus environments, many of which were already linked to conventional residencies and clinical training experiences.

Clarifying the core competencies of integrative medicine

A second, multidisciplinary survey was stimulated by the response of ACCAHC participants to the publication of a CAHCIM-endorsed paper in *Academic Medicine* on competencies in integrative medicine (Kligler et al., 2004). The paper was developed internally by CAHCIM, without input from leaders of the ACCAHC disciplines. A modified Delphi survey administered to a subset of 18 complementary healthcare educators representing all the ACCAHC core disciplines eventually elicited five key areas of concern with the competencies endorsed by CAHCIM (Benjamin et al., 2007). Most of the concerns relevant to the core issue of integration were not focused solely on therapies, but on an active engagement between diverse disciplines. The survey found that:

- The CAHCIM paper leaves the impression that conventional medical physicians may simply incorporate into their practices what they perceive to be good CAM therapies rather than referring to or co-managing and collaborating with CAM providers.
- The CAHCIM paper does not include the option of integrated care with MDs and CAM practitioners as partners, and seems to propose that CAM be an add-on to conventional medical care.
- Occasionally in the paper language appears to reflect a continuation of the 'us and them' mindset rather than seeing that CAM providers, faculty, and systems could and should be part of IM.
- The paper gives the impression that conventional medical institutions want to include CAM, but not necessarily CAM practitioners, in their vision of IM.
- CAM is defined in relationship to biomedicine as complementary or alternative, but is considered integrative if delivered by conventional physicians. (Benjamin et al., p. 1023)

The issue of the distinction between integration of therapies versus the more challenging and the significantly more beneficial work of collaboration between disciplines led to a process in which CAHCIM changed its definition of integrative medicine to better reflect the importance of working with other disciplines (see Sidebar 2.1)

Efforts to create shared values to guide interdisciplinary action
A third project, led by holistic nurse educator Carla Mariano, EdD, RN, AHN-BC, FAAIM, sought to clarify a shared set of values

Sidebar 2.1

From Integration of Therapies to Collaboration among Disciplines

The planning team for the National Education Dialogue (NED) to Advance Integrated Health Care: *Creating Common Ground* was an alphabet soup of titles never before gathered for a shared educational purpose, including MD, ND (naturopathic physician), LAc (acupuncture and Oriental medicine practitioner), MPH, DC (doctor of chiropractic), PhD, LM (licensed midwife), RN, LMT (licensed massage therapist), and RYT (registered yoga teacher).

The hope and expectation among educators and practitioners was that such educational collaboration would translate into more understanding and greater cooperation among practitioners. The organizing mantra was *those who learn together practice together.* What could educators do to help get their disciplines out of separate silos and break down the historic barriers between conventional and alternative professions? An early step was to clarify the shared vision, if any, unifying the leaders. The group agreed on this statement:

> We envision a healthcare system that is multidisciplinary and enhances competence, mutual respect and collaboration across all complementary and alternative medicine and conventional healthcare disciplines. This system will deliver effective care that is patient centered, focused on health creation and healing, and readily accessible to all populations (Weeks et al., 2005; p. 1).

A funny thing happened on the way to working on this vision. On the December 2004 NED planning team call, one of these planners announced that at the recent general meeting of CAHCIM, the conventionally-based academics had agreed on a definition of integrative medicine.

> Integrative medicine is the practice of medicine that reaffirms the importance of the relationship between practitioner and patient, focuses on the whole person, is informed by evidence, and makes use of all appropriate therapeutic approaches to achieve optimal health and healing (Weeks et al., 2005: p.16).

The successful agreement among representatives from the 25 medical schools on a definition of their field had taken months of committee work. The eight members of the NED planning team who also were members of CAHCIM were congratulated.

But this definition was not well received by many on the call. The first issue was participatory: if integrative medicine was intended to be inclusive, then why were leaders of other disciplines not asked to collaborate on establishing the definition? The second issue was substantive and went to the heart of collaboration. Where, in that definition, was the evidence that a practitioner of integrative medicine must, in the words of the NED vision, be "multidisciplinary and enhance(s) competence, mutual respect and collaboration across all complementary and alternative medicine and conventional health care disciplines?"

One responsibility that ACCAHC had in the NED process was to articulate and advance shared issues relating to the cultural-medical shift toward more integrated health care. That the definition of integrative medicine included no reference to the importance of knowing how to collaborate with other types of healthcare professionals and disciplines was one issue. There were others. The word "approach," for instance, did not appropriately characterize the unique contributions of practitioners licensed in the 4000-year-old discipline of acupuncture and Oriental medicine.

ACCAHC members asked their CAHCIM colleagues to change their definition of integrative medicine. The request was well received. A conventional colleague noted that the Institute of Medicine of the National Academies, in its *Report on Complementary and Alternative Medicine in the United States*, had underscored the importance of care that is "collaborative and interdisciplinary and that respects and joins effective interventions from all sources." The CAHCIM definition was formally amended to read:

> Integrative medicine is the practice of medicine that reaffirms the importance of the relationship between practitioner and patient, focuses on the whole person, is informed by evidence, and makes use of all appropriate therapeutic approaches, **healthcare professionals and disciplines** to achieve optimal health and healing. [Amendments in bold.] (Weeks et al., 2005; p.16)

In short, integrative medicine requires more than integration of specific therapeutic approaches. This definition was used widely in the 2009 Institute of Medicine Summit on Integrative Medicine and the Health of the Public. Practitioners must also know how to make the best use of other healthcare professionals and disciplines to achieve optimal health and healing. Notably, the amended definition also elevated the status of all nonmedical, nonCAM disciplines including nurses, physical therapists, psychologists, nutritionists, and others. A definitional platform was laid for an emerging vision of an integrated healthcare system that will require all disciplines to recognize that they must work as part of respectful, collaborative teams.

A brief coda: Several years of living with the definition have revealed one other area where some in the complementary healthcare community might prefer an additional amendment. While the definition does not say that it only refers to practice by medical doctors, many read the definition as MD-centric. Clarity that it is the "practice of medicine, *by members of any discipline*" would be a more inclusive framing.

across the disciplines involved with the NED process. The vision behind this project was of a document that might be co-produced by a multidisciplinary NED team and endorsed by the NED planning committee and then amended and endorsed by the onsite gathering of 75 educators. If agreement were reached, the document could then be taken to the individual disciplines for endorsement as a shared basis for interdisciplinary action. The operating belief of the 10 educators from eight disciplines who comprised the Values, Knowledge, Skills and Attitudes Task Force was that the process of shifting the disciplines out of their historic isolation would benefit from a collaboratively-developed guiding document.

Through a series of phone meetings, a small work group created a draft statement of core values. These were coupled with examples of knowledge and skills associated with each of the values. The Task Force as a group endorsed the statements as a working document. The core values served as the basis of an intensely interactive World Café format for the 75 educators at the onsite NED meeting. (See the text of the draft document in Sidebar 2.2.) The participants at the gathering proved to be a long way from consensus on the document. There were contradictory feelings about the ultimate contribution such a document might have, even though an onsite survey strongly supported continuing the work "to create a concise statement of core values which have resonance across the disciplines and can guide efforts to create quality integrated healthcare education."

A reconstituted Task Force continued work via a series of phone meetings after the onsite meeting. They found two resources of particular value in guiding their activity together. One was the section on Practitioner to Practitioner Relationships in the Pew-Fetzer seminal document on relationship-centered care (Tresolini, 1994; p. 36). (Further information on the report's findings is provided in Table 2.3.) Particularly noteworthy were issues related to knowledge of self, ability to understand the "historical power inequities across the professions," "affirmation of the value of diversity," and the importance of team dynamics.

The second guiding document for the team's work was the Four Quadrants from Ken Wilbur's *Integral Theory of Consciousness* (Wilbur, 1997). The group quickly noticed that much of the integration activity has been shaped by the right quadrants, which are related to exterior inputs such as randomized controlled trials, publications,

Table 2.3

**Practitioner to Practitioner Relationships
in Relationship-Centered Care***

Area	Knowledge	Skills	Values
Self awareness	• Knowledge of self	• Reflect on self and needs • Learn continuously	• Importance of self-awareness
Traditions of knowledge in health professions	• Healing approaches of various professions and across cultures • Historical power inequities across professions	• Derive meaning from others' work • Learn from experience in a healing community	• Affirmation and value of diversity
Building teams and communities	• Perspectives on team building from the social sciences	• Communicate effectively • Listen openly • Learn cooperatively	• Affirmation of mission • Affirmation of diversity
Working dynamics of teams and communities	• Perspectives on team dynamics from the social sciences	• Share responsibility responsibly • Collaborate with others • Work cooperatively • Resolve conflicts	• Openness to others' ideas • Humility • Mutual trust, empathy, support • Capacity for grace

*Source: Tresolini C.P. and the Pew-Fetzer Task Force. *Health Professions Education and Relationship-Centered Care.* San Francisco, CA: Pew Health Professions Commission. 1994; p. 36. ©Pew Health Commission and the Fetzer Institute.

and capacity to participate. The Values Working Group engaged an internal process to explore the way that subjective issues such as self-knowledge, personal involvement in health, and appreciation of the diversity of professional experience and culture influence collaborative behavior.

Model Education Tools on the Disciplines

We recognize that expanding and strengthening integration and collaboration will require some remedial education. Practitioners of one healthcare system cannot effectively collaborate with practitioners of other systems unless they first possess accurate and adequate knowledge of and understanding about the various healthcare disciplines that exist. (This book reflects one effort

Sidebar 2.2

Toward Core Values to Shape
Collaboration in Integrated Care

Note: A multidisciplinary team of educators from eight disciplines collaborated in a series of conference calls to propose the following as a set of values to guide disciplines in working toward integrated health care. While never formally endorsed by the disciplines involved in the National Education Dialogue meeting, these remain a good framework for collaboration.

Wholeness and Healing
We acknowledge and value the interconnectedness of all people and all things. We believe that healing is an innate, although sometimes mysterious, capacity of every individual, which provides a meaningful opportunity for growth and balance, even when curing may not be possible.

Clients/Patients/Families
We value our clients/patients/families as the center of our practices. We act in service to validate individuals' full experience of their wellness and illness, provide education about the possibilities for change, diminish dependence, bolster resilience, support the mobilization of their full resources, and reinforce self-reliance as important to optimal healing.

Practice as Combined Art and Science
We value competent, compassionate, relationship-centered practice that honors intuitive knowledge, stimulates creativity in the face of divergent circumstances, and appropriately utilizes a network of diverse practitioners as integral to the practice of the healing arts. This approach is informed by in-depth education, critical thinking, reliable evidence from well-designed quantitative and qualitative research, and by respect for diverse theories and world views.

Self-Care of the Practitioner
We value a practitioner's commitment to self-reflection, self-care, and to his or her personal growth and healing as being essential to one's humble ability to provide the most effective and enduring health care to others.

Interdisciplinary Collaboration and Integration
We embrace the breadth and depth of diverse healthcare systems and value collaboration of all providers within and across disciplines and with clients/patients and their families. We believe that fostering integrative and collaborative practice is essential to the creation of health, the advancement of health care, and the well-being of society.

Our Health System
We value the recognition that all practitioners have responsibility to participate in activities which contribute to the improvement of the community, the environment, and the betterment of public health. We support access for all populations to competent client/patient-centered care, which is focused on health creation and healing. We believe that advancement and promotion of health and the prevention of disease are fostered by aligning resource investment with these values.

Attitudes and Behaviors that Promote Health, Wellness, and Change
We value attitudes and behaviors which demonstrate respect for self and others and which are informed by an abiding humility, in light of both the individual care and system challenges which we face. We value authentic, open, and courageous communication. We believe that such traits are important for all participants in health care, whether practitioner, client/patient/family, educator, administrator, or policy-maker.

Source: Developed through an ACCAHC and National Education Dialogue team chaired by Carla Mariano, RN, EdD, BC-HN and including Michael Goldstein, PhD, Ben Kligler, MD, MPH, Karen Lawson, MD, David O'Bryon, JD, Mark Seem, LAc, Dawn Schmidt, LMP, Pamela Snider, ND, Don Warren, ND, DHANP, and John Weeks.

to correct shortcomings.) The decades of separation between conventional and complementary healthcare disciplines, between the mind and body, and between the physical locations of our educational institutions and clinics, underscore the importance of such education. A well-formulated survey course, or set of courses, would provide an important basis for opening hearts and minds to the "other," with the ultimate and critical goal of serving patients more effectively.

There are numerous strategies to enhance collaboration and to train all practitioners about disciplines other than their own. Dialogue is vital. As practitioners become better able to discuss healthcare options outside of their own fields with both patients and other practitioners, they can better understand treatments patients may already be receiving from other healthcare practitioners. Cross-referral will be enhanced as practitioners develop openness to other medical cultures and paradigms. The potential to work successfully in multidisciplinary healthcare settings and on collaborative research projects will be enhanced.

Sidebar 2.3 presents a brief overview of suggested topics and formats for educating conventional medical students about the CAM disciplines. It is based on work led by Elizabeth Goldblatt PhD, MPA/HA and Daniel Seitz, JD, involving a team of eight professionals from four disciplines; the information was presented at the NED onsite gathering. To transmit adequate knowledge in an academic setting, representatives of each discipline recommended at least 2–3 credits or 30–45 course hours on each discipline. However, already bulging educational requirements in all the health professions schools effectively vetoed such an approach. A compromise recommendation, though still a challenge to fit, is a survey course of 30–45 contact hours in which all of the licensed complementary healthcare disciplines are examined. Recognizing that even this is a push for many educational programs, ACCAHC hopes that this *Desk Reference* will help to increase general knowledge of the licensed alternative and complementary health professions and provide a resource for such a course.

Priority Recommendations for Interdisciplinary Educational Collaboration

After 15 months of planning and collaborative project execution, three days onsite, and two surveys of participants, the National

Sidebar 2.3

Topics and Suggested Formats in Education on the Distinctly Licensed Complementary and Alternative Healthcare Professions

Educational topics

- Basic philosophy about health and healing
- Core values of the discipline
- Basic theory of the discipline and any unique terminology
- History and current status of the field
- Status of research in the field, review of the literature, evidence-based material, cultural issues that may restrict or enhance research, and research priorities identified by the profession
- Strengths and limitations in preventing and treating illness and promoting health
- Educational training requirements, competencies
- Institutional and programmatic accreditation practices
- Certification and examination agencies and processes
- Professional licensing and scope of practice
- Credentialing issues in hospitals and third-party payment
- Experience in co-management and referral strategies
- Best practices in integration with other practitioners
- Bibliography of recommended additional resources

Activities and educational formats

- Lecture and demonstrations on how the discipline approaches specific cases (best practices, strengths/weaknesses, working alone, working collaboratively)
- Joint case discussions in which specific cases are presented from the perspectives of a variety of disciplines
- Direct experience of different forms of healthcare, such as receiving acupuncture and Oriental medicine treatments, chiropractic adjustments, nutrition and diet assessments, massage therapy, and the whole person naturopathic intake
- Grand rounds presentations in integrative clinics
- Present a few simple techniques that can be incorporated into self-care
- Explore how to work collaboratively and co-manage cases with other healthcare providers

Based on materials developed by Elizabeth (Liza) Goldblatt, PhD, MPA/HA and Daniel Seitz, JD, MAT, with the ACCAHC and NED team, which also included Frank Zolli, DC, EdD, Adam Perlman, MD, Pamela Snider, ND, Don Warren, ND, and John Weeks.

Education Dialogue to Advance Integrated Health Care identified nine priority areas for action in which there was significant common ground (>80% agreement) (Weeks et al., 2005; p. 3).

- Facilitate development of inter-institutional relationships and geographically-based groupings of conventional and CAM institutions and disciplines in diverse regions. Promote student and faculty exchanges, create new clinical opportunities, facilitate integrated postgraduate and residency programs, and provide opportunities for students to audit classes and share library privileges.
- Create resource modules on teaching about distinct CAM, conventional, and emerging disciplines (approved by the disciplines), which can be used in a variety of formats—from supporting materials in such areas as definitions and glossaries to full curricular modules.
- Share educational and faculty resources and information on inter-institutional relationships, including samples of existing agreements and existing educational resources through development of a website.
- Continue multidisciplinary work to create a concise statement of core values that have resonance across the disciplines and can guide efforts to create quality integrated healthcare education.
- Collaboratively develop and sponsor continuing education initiatives designed to draw participants from diverse disciplines.
- Create collaboratively developed educational resources to prepare students and practitioners to practice in integrated clinical settings.
- Develop an outline of skills and attitudes appropriate for those involved in collaborative integrated health care.
- Assist individuals with making institutional changes by offering support for leadership in change creation. Explore strategies for overcoming the challenges of prejudice, ignorance and cultural diversity.
- Explore third-party clinical sites that serve the underserved (such as community health centers) as locations for developing clinical education in integrated healthcare practices.

Collaboration following the NED meeting

Significant efforts were made to find philanthropic support that would allow the NED work groups to remain intact and begin addressing these priorities. Limited funds were raised to advance the values initiative and some interdisciplinary collaboration, but unfortunately the broader NED effort had to be suspended roughly a year later. The effort's epitaph was provided while NED was still robust by the chair of the Institute of Medicine committee that produced the 2005 report on complementary and alternative health care in the US: "What you are doing [with NED], this great collaborative work, is one of the most important things anyone can do to implement this report." (Weeks et al., 2005: p.1)

Activity to advance the collaborative agenda has continued on many fronts. Leaders of ACCAHC chose to take what was originally a project of the IHPC and create an independent organization as a basis for ongoing interdisciplinary action. As noted in the introduction, ACCAHC was formally incorporated in 2008 and has gathered increased participation from leaders of the licensed complementary healthcare professions as well as Traditional World Medicines organizations which are engaging self-regulatory and regulatory efforts. (See the Introduction for more information.)

Cross-fertilization between the CAHCIM and ACCAHC has also continued. Executive teams met in 2006, and, in 2009, as noted above, roughly 95 leaders, evenly split between the two organizations, met for a half day to explore formal collaboration on various projects. The infrastructure for collaboration represented by these two organizations is expected to bear significant fruit in coming years.

Summary

The past decade has seen significant development of the values, definitional commitments, and operational infrastructure needed to support collaborative action and prepare the way for an integrated healthcare system. Conventional medicine, integrative medicine, and the licensed complementary and alternative healthcare professions must all continue to work on that goal for many years to come.

Collaborative action is already expanding despite the historic estrangement between many of these fields. An ongoing challenge is to show how patients can benefit when practitioners of different stripes are not merely viewed as purveyors of therapies but as exponents of entire disciplines with their own rich histories and distinct approaches to patient care. Strategies for enriching cross-disciplinary experiences in the midst of already excessive curriculum requirements must be developed. To be urging additional coursework and clinical exposures on heavily burdened health professions students puts all of us in an uncomfortable position. Yet multiple forces in the broader culture energize this effort. These range from cultural shifts and consumer interests to top level reports on the importance of collaboration in the treatment of costly chronic diseases. Patient-centered care, patient-practitioner partnerships, and team medicine are all elements of renewed efforts to create a medical system which is proactive and focused on health creation.

A frequently quoted opinion among academic researchers concerning integrative and complementary healthcare themes is that one day we will no longer have conventional medicine and alternative medicine, but only good medicine. Such a rosy resolution of the philosophical debates on diverse approaches to health and medicine that go back not just decades but centuries cannot be expected in the near future. However, we can all learn to collaborate more respectfully and effectively despite our differences, and that is certainly a part of good medicine and very likely a necessary antecedent to greater success overall.

The subsequent chapters in this Desk Reference concern the disciplines themselves and should make a significant contribution to a shared understanding of the characteristics, practices, and strengths of these fields.

Bibliography

Benjamin PJ, Phillips R, Warren D, et al. Response to a proposal for an integrative medicine curriculum. *J Altern Complent Med*. 2007;13:1021-1033.

Center for the Health Professions at University of California San Francisco Web site. http://futurehealth.ucsf.edu/Content/2/1994-12_Health_Professions_ Education_and_Relationship-centered_Care.pdf. Accessed August 24, 2008.

Eisenberg DM, Davis RB, Ettner SL, et al. Trends in alternative medicine use in the United States, 1990-1997. *JAMA*. 1998;280:1569-1575.

Eisenberg DM, Kessler RC, Foster C, Norlock FE, Calkins DR, Delbanco TL. Unconventional medicine in the United States. Prevalence, costs, and patterns of use. *N Engl J Med*. 1993;328:246-252.

http://www.imprint.co.uk/Wilber.htm. Accessed August 24, 2008.

Institute of Medicine of the National Academies, Committee on the Use of Complementary and Alternative Medicine by the American Public, Board on Health Promotion and Disease Prevention. *Complementary and Alternative Medicine in the United States*. Washington, DC: National Academies Press; 2005.

Kligler B, Maizes V, Schachter S, et al. Core competencies in integrative medicine for medical school curricula: a proposal. *Acad Med*. 2004;79:521-531.

National Institutes of Health. *White House Commission on Complementary and Alternative Medicine Policy*. NIH Publication 03-5411. Washington, DC: US Government Printing Office; 2003.

Nedrow AR, Heitkemper M, Frenkel M, Mann D, Wayne P, Hughes E. Collaborations between allopathic and complementary and alternative medicine health professionals: four initiatives. *Acad Med*. 2007;82:962-966.

Quinn S, Traub M, eds. *National Policy Dialogue to Advance Integrated Health Care: Finding Common Ground*. Seattle, WA: Integrated Healthcare Policy Consortium; 2002. http://ihpc.info/resources/NPDFR.pdf. Accessed August 24, 2008.

Tresolini CP and the Pew-Fetzer Task Force. Health Professions Education and Relationship-Centered Care. San Francisco, CA: Pew Health Professions Commission; 1994:36.

Weeks J, Snider P, Quinn S, O'Bryon D, Haramati A. National Education Dialogue to Advance Integrated Health Care: Creating Common Ground. Progress Report, March 2004-September 2005. Integrated Healthcare Policy Consortium Web site. http://ihpc.info/resources/NEDPR.pdf. Accessed August 24, 2008.

Weeks J. The future of MD education: empathy, roses and respect via Georgetown and U Minnesota pilots. *The Integrator Blog News & Report*. August 15, 2006. The Integrator Blog Web site. http://theintegratorblog.com/site/index.php?option=com_content&task=view&id=128&Itemid=93. Accessed August 24, 2008.

Wilbur K. An integral theory of consciousness. *J Consciousness Studies* 1997;4(1): 71-92.

Section III

Licensed Complementary and Alternative Healthcare Professions

Acupuncture and Oriental Medicine

Chiropractic

Massage Therapy

Direct-entry Midwifery

Naturopathic Medicine

Acupuncture and Oriental Medicine

David Sale, JD, LLM, Steve Given, DAOM, LAc,
Catherine Niemiec, JD, LAc, Elizabeth Goldblatt, PhD, MPA/HA

Partner Organization: Council of Colleges of Acupuncture
and Oriental Medicine (CCAOM)

About the Authors: Sale is executive director of the CCAOM. Given is vice president of the CCAOM and associate dean and director of the doctorate program in the School of Acupuncture & Oriental Medicine at Bastyr University. Niemiec is an institutional member of the Accreditation Commission for Acupuncture and Oriental Medicine and is president of the Phoenix Institute of Herbal Medicine and Acupuncture. Goldblatt is past president of CCAOM, vice president for academic affairs of the American College for Traditional Chinese Medicine, and chair of ACCAHC.

Philosophy, Mission, Goals

The history of acupuncture and Oriental medicine (AOM) extends back over 3000 years, with documentation of accumulated knowledge and experience appearing before the Han Dynasty (206 BCE to 220 CE), thus providing a long record of traditional use. Since the 1970s, AOM has experienced increasing popularity in the US.

The philosophy of this ancient therapeutic system is based on the concept of *qi* (pronounced "chee"), meaning energy/life force, and its flow through the body along channels or meridians. This ancient medicine has its own nomenclature, physiology, pathology, and therapeutics, which create a complex system of medicine.

Practitioners, educators, and national AOM organizations seek to promote a variety of complementary goals. These include: standards of excellence, competence, and integrity in the practice of the profession; public safety; excellence in AOM education; high quality health care; integration of AOM into the US healthcare system; use of acupuncture as an adjunctive treatment for addictions and mental disorders; assistance to communities affected by disaster,

war, conflict, and poverty; the uniqueness and credibility of acupuncture through research; regulatory collaboration among AOM
state administrative boards; and Asian bodywork therapy.

Characteristics and Data

Prior to the 1970s, AOM was practiced in the US within Asian
communities that arose after the completion of the Transcontinen-
tal Railroad in the 1840s. Acupuncture experienced a renaissance
in the US in the early 1970s. Interest was heightened when James
Reston, a newspaper columnist for the *New York Times*, wrote an
article about the benefits of acupuncture he received during his
recovery from an appendectomy in China when former President
Nixon made his historic visit to China in 1971 (*New York Times*,
July 26, 1971). The following four major acupuncture institutions
were formed in the early 1980s:

- Council of Colleges of Acupuncture and Oriental Medicine
  (CCAOM), the voluntary national membership association
  for AOM schools
- Accreditation Commission for Acupuncture and Oriental Medicine (ACAOM), the US Department of Education-
  recognized national accrediting organization for AOM
  schools
- National Certification Commission for Acupuncture and
  Oriental Medicine (NCCAOM), the national testing organization for certifying competency in AOM
- American Association of Acupuncture and Oriental Medicine (AAAOM), the national professional association of AOM
  practitioners

There are approximately 20,000–25,000 AOM licensees throughout the US. While current data concerning the income of these
practitioners nationwide is not available, recent estimates have
suggested an annual salary range of $30,000-$60,000. However, it
is not uncommon for practitioners to earn in excess of this amount,
with reported salaries in some instances exceeding $100,000.

There are approximately 8,000 students enrolled in AOM programs in the US. In the early years of the profession in the US, students were primarily those looking for a second career. Increasingly,
students today are looking to the AOM field as a first career.

Clinical Care

Approach to patient care

Treatments provided by AOM practitioners identify a pattern of disharmony within a patient and redress that disharmony in a variety of ways that may include any or all of the tools of Oriental medicine. AOM seeks to achieve balance through the application of opposite energetic forces (e.g., clear heat through administration of cooling herbal formulas or acupuncture points specifically noted for their ability to release heat from the body) or through the strengthening of weak or deficient areas. The AOM practitioner typically proceeds by observing signs and symptoms that comprise a pattern of disharmony and one's constitutional state, rather than by developing a biomedical diagnosis based on etiologic assessments. AOM is used for chronic disease, prevention and wellness, and acute care. It is appropriate for in-depth individual care as well as for simultaneous treatment of large groups of people, such as treatment of emergency care workers at the site of 9/11 and Hurricane Katrina, or drug offenders in addiction recovery groups.

Practitioners of AOM approach patients from a holistic perspective, taking into account all aspects of their health, recognizing the interconnectedness of the mind, emotions, and body, as well as the environment. When *qi* is stagnant or out of balance, which can result from natural, physical or emotional causes, illness and premature aging can occur. Oriental medicine involves a variety of techniques to restore balance to *qi* that has become stagnant or imbalanced, including acupuncture and related therapies (various needle techniques and tools, cupping, *gwa sha* or scraping technique, moxibustion, modern use of electrical and cold laser therapy); Asian forms of massage such as acupressure, shiatsu, and tuina; herbal medicine; exercise (*tai qi* and *qi gong*); Oriental dietary therapy; and meditation. Methods of diagnosis include the ability to interpret topography of the tongue, palpation of pulse and acupuncture points, and extensive observation and interpretation of all bodily symptoms and physical features according to Oriental medical physiology. This medicine is used to treat a broad range of illnesses ranging from rehabilitation and pain management to virally mediated disorders and neurological complaints. There are several styles of Oriental medicine, including Traditional Chinese Medicine (TCM), Worsley/5-element theory, Japanese meridian theory, French Energetics, and Korean hand therapy.

Practitioners generally spend a significant amount of time developing a collaborative relationship with their patients, assisting them in maintaining their health and promoting a consciousness of wellness. As a relatively cost-effective form of treatment, AOM may be especially appropriate for reducing healthcare costs and improving access to care. It is also very safe, resulting in very rare unintended events.

Scope of practice

The scope of practice for AOM varies considerably from state to state. Acupuncture is frequently defined as the stimulation of certain points on or near the surface of the human body by the insertion of needles to prevent or modify the perception of pain, to normalize physiological functions, or to treat certain diseases or dysfunctions of the body. A number of state statutes reference the *energetic* aspect of acupuncture by noting its usefulness in controlling and regulating the flow and balance of *qi* in the body or in normalizing energetic physiological function. Other state statutes may define acupuncture by reference to traditional or modern Chinese or Oriental medical concepts or to modern techniques of diagnostic evaluation.

State laws may also specifically authorize acupuncture licensees to employ a wide panoply of AOM therapies such as moxibustion, cupping, Oriental or therapeutic massage, therapeutic exercise, electroacupuncture, acupressure, dietary recommendations, herbal therapy, injection and laser therapy, ion cord devices, magnets, *qi gong*, and massage. The treatment of animals, the ordering of western diagnostic tests, and the use of homeopathy are, with limitations, within the scope of practice in some states.

Referral practices

AOM practitioners receive training in biomedicine, including training on appropriate referrals to medical practitioners. Some states specify the process for referral, but in most cases medical referral is determined by the AOM practitioner. Conversely, patients seeking AOM practitioners are mostly self-referred or referred by word of mouth. Some states specify that medical referral is required for a patient to be seen by an AOM practitioner.

Patients may be referred to professional acupuncturists for a variety of complaints. While the list below is not comprehensive, it represents the typical array of complaints for which referral to an acupuncturist is quite appropriate:

1. Pain management, including musculoskeletal pain, rheumatological or oncological pain, headache/migraine, and pain palliation at end of life
2. Neurogenic pain, including neuropathy associated with diabetes mellitus, chemotherapy, and the neuropathy associated with antiretroviral therapy
3. Women's health, including dysmenorrhea, premenstrual syndrome, amenorrhea, infertility, and pain associated with endometriosis
4. Nausea and vomiting associated with pregnancy, chemotherapy-induced nausea, and postoperative nausea
5. The symptoms associated with virally mediated disorders, including HIV, the hepatitis viruses, and the pain associated with herpes zoster and herpes simplex I and II
6. Neurological disorders, including Bell's palsy, cerebral vascular accident, and multiple sclerosis
7. Routine infections such as colds and flu
8. Dermatological complaints, such as dermatitis and psoriasis
9. Gastrointestinal complaints, including gastralgia, inflammatory bowel disease, irritable bowel syndrome, and gastroesophageal reflux disease
10. Respiratory complaints, including mild to moderate asthma, shortness of breath, and cough
11. Urogenital complaints, including dysurea, cystitis, and impotence
12. Mild to moderate anxiety and depression
13. Chemical dependency, including abuse of opiates and sympathomimetics
14. Fatigue secondary to chronic illness, medical treatment, or surgery

In 2003, a World Health Organization study, *Acupuncture: Review and Analysis of Reports on Controlled Clinical Trials*, cited over 43 conditions that are treatable with acupuncture.

Third-party payers

Increasingly, acupuncture is covered in many insurance plans, is reimbursed by other third-party payers for certain conditions, and is a part of many employer programs. For the most part, however, payments to individual providers are made by the patient. Indeed, AOM has grown within the US through word of mouth and referrals based on successful treatments and is increasingly recognized as a safe, effective medicine in a wide variety of settings including general health care, integrative medical practices, hospitals, spas and medispa practices, sports and fitness gyms, nonprofit community clinics, and addiction and recovery programs. There remains, however, a significant disparity in traditional insurance coverage compared to other healthcare professions that have been established in the mainstream world of insurance reimbursement for several decades.

Legislation requiring the coverage of acupuncture services under federal Medicare and the Federal Employee Benefits Program (FEBP) has been introduced in Congress for a number of years and is under consideration in the current congress in H.R. 646 (Federal Acupuncture Coverage Act of 2009). The enactment of such legislation has long enjoyed significant support from within the profession. It has been estimated that approximately one-fourth of the insurance plans in the FEBP offer acupuncture benefits and that nearly 75% of the federal work force is covered by plans offering acupuncture. These plans, however, offer such coverage only on a voluntary basis and, in some instances, only if the acupuncture services are provided by a medical doctor or doctor of osteopathy.

Integration Activities

Interest in training that prepares AOM students to work in integrative healthcare settings is high among CCAOM's 54 AOM member institutions. A substantial number of these colleges offer internships in over 100 off-site clinics where AOM services are provided in local communities. These clinics include a variety of settings, including hospitals, multi-specialty centers, research-based centers, long- and short-term rehabilitation centers, family practice clinics, nursing homes, outpatient geriatric or assisted living centers for seniors, drug treatment centers, HIV/AIDS treatment facilities, sports medicine clinics, pediatric, cancer, and other specialty care centers, and clinics addressing specific community group needs, such as women's health and inner city/low income/multi-racial groups.

In addition, CCAOM actively participates in the work of the Academic Consortium for Complementary and Alternative Health Care whose work, in collaboration with leaders from conventional medical educational institutions, has focused on developing strategies for integrating conventional and CAM education.

Education

Schools and programs

The first acupuncture school in the US was established in 1975. In 1982, the Council of Colleges of Acupuncture and Oriental Medicine (CCAOM) was founded as a nonprofit, voluntary membership association for AOM colleges and programs. Currently the membership of the CCAOM consists of 54 member schools, all of which have achieved accreditation, or are candidates for accreditation, with the Accreditation Commission for Acupuncture and Oriental Medicine (ACAOM), the national accrediting agency for AOM schools. This membership is spread over some 21 states, with major concentrations of colleges in California, New York, and Florida. There is significant diversity in the programs among CCAOM's member schools with representation of the Traditional Chinese Medicine, Japanese, Five Element, Korean, and Vietnamese traditions. The growth of CCAOM since the early years of its founding, when there were fewer than 12 member schools, has mirrored the general growth of the profession.

The mission of CCAOM is to advance AOM by promoting educational excellence in the field. In furtherance of this mission, the goals of CCAOM as formally stated in its bylaws are:

- to support the development and improvement of educational programs in acupuncture and Oriental medicine
- to develop recommended curricula for degree, diploma, and other educational programs
- to support and foster academic freedom and a diversity of educational approaches within the field
- to encourage scientific research, innovative teaching methodology, and faculty development
- to provide a forum for discussion of issues relevant to member colleges

- to serve as an information resource for member colleges, other colleges and organizations, regulatory agencies, and the public
- to encourage ethical business practices among member colleges
- to work with accreditation, certification, licensing, and other regulatory agencies to develop appropriate educational standards and requirements
- to promote increased public access to high quality health care provided by well-trained practitioners of acupuncture and Oriental medicine

The Executive Committee of the CCAOM consists of eight officers who are full-time presidents, CEOs, program directors, or other administrators at CCAOM's member schools. The full CCAOM meets twice each year in meetings that provide a forum for member institutions to dialogue about issues of importance to the colleges. In addition, CCAOM's meetings provide an opportunity for its many committees to meet face-to-face and for the membership to benefit from panel discussions, strategic planning, and specialized workshops.

The CCAOM does much of its work through a committee structure, including committees concerned with clean needle technique, core curriculum, distance education, entry-level standards, ethics, faculty development, finance, herbs, libraries, marketing/public relations, membership, emergency preparedness, research information, and special needs. The CCAOM also administers a national needle safety program for new AOM graduates (CNT Course).

Curriculum content

The entry-level standard of training and education for the profession is the master's degree, which is typically a 3-4 year program that offers either the first-professional master's degree or the first-professional master's level certificate or diploma. Under ACAOM's national accreditation standards, AOM institutions that offer a master's degree in acupuncture must be at least 3 academic years in length and provide a minimum of 1905 hours of a professional acupuncture curriculum over a three-year period (typically taken over four calendar years). The curriculum for an acupuncture program must consist of at least 705 didactic hours in Oriental medical theory, diagnosis, and treatment techniques in acupuncture and related studies; 660 hours in clinical training; 450 hours in biomedical clinical sciences; and 90 hours in counseling, communication, ethics and practice management.

A professional Oriental medicine curriculum, which is a minimum of four academic years and includes training in acupuncture and the additional study of Chinese herbal medicine, must consist of at least 2625 hours leading to a master's degree or master's level certificate or diploma in Oriental medicine. The curriculum for an Oriental medicine program must consist of at least 705 hours in Oriental medical theory, diagnosis, and treatment techniques in acupuncture and related studies; 450 hours in didactic Oriental herbal studies; 870 hours in integrated acupuncture and herbal clinical training; 510 hours in biomedical clinical sciences; and 90 hours in counseling, communication, ethics, and practice management.

For some years, there has been an ongoing dialogue within the profession concerning the amount of academic training a person needs to practice AOM at the entry level and what the most appropriate professional title should be for providers. This dialogue has been formally focused within a doctoral task force established by ACAOM, whose work is discussed in more detail in this chapter under the heading of Accreditation. The average number of academic hours of study and training associated with the entry-level Master's degree among AOM colleges nationally is between 2,700 and 2,900 hours. A significant number of Oriental medicine programs have a curriculum of 3,000 hours or more. The trend over the years has been for an increase in the number of academic hours.

As of the summer of 2009, ACAOM had approved 9 colleges to offer postgraduate clinical doctoral programs on a pilot basis (3 have achieved accreditation and 2 had candidacy status for this degree). The degree for this program, titled Doctorate in Acupuncture & Oriental Medicine (DAOM), may provide advanced training in either acupuncture or in Oriental medicine. DAOM programs must provide advanced didactic and clinical training in one or more clinical specialty areas in AOM. Completion of a master's degree or master's-level program in acupuncture or in Oriental medicine is a prerequisite for admission to a DAOM program. Such programs must comprise a minimum of 1200 hours of advanced AOM training in one or more clinical specialty areas at the doctoral level. As of December 31, 2012, a majority of the faculty must possess a doctoral degree, the terminal degree, or its international equivalent in the subject areas in which the faculty teach. Clinical supervisors should have a minimum of five years of documented professional experience as licensed Oriental medicine practitioners.

Faculty and other training information

The accreditation standards for master's level programs as prescribed by ACAOM specify general requirements for AOM faculty. Thus, AOM faculty must be academically qualified and numerically sufficient to perform their responsibilities. Additionally, the general education, professional education, teaching experience, and practical professional experience of faculty must be appropriate for the subject area taught. Faculty members must also provide continuing evidence of keeping abreast of developments in the fields and subjects in which they teach.

Accreditation

ACAOM was established in 1982 and is the only national accrediting body recognized by the US Department of Education as a reliable authority for quality education and training in AOM. Its current scope of recognition with the USDE is the "...accreditation and preaccreditation ("Candidacy") throughout the US of first-professional master's degree and professional master's level certificate and diploma programs in AOM, as well as free-standing institutions and colleges of AOM that offer such programs...." As an accrediting agency, ACAOM's primary purposes are to establish comprehensive educational and institutional requirements for acupuncture and Oriental medicine programs, to accredit programs and institutions that meet these requirements, and to foster excellence in acupuncture and Oriental medicine through the implementation of accreditation standards for AOM educational institutions and programs.

ACAOM was first recognized by the US Department of Education (USDE) in 1988 for the accreditation of master's degree and master's-level acupuncture programs. In 1992, ACAOM was granted an expansion of scope by the USDE to include the accreditation of programs in Oriental medicine, which are programs that include the study of Chinese herbal medicine. In May 2006, the USDE renewed ACAOM's recognition for USDE's maximum five-year period. The establishment of ACAOM and its recognition by USDE have made it possible for AOM students to obtain federal student loans for their education. When the USDE renewed ACAOM's recognition in 2006, the federal agency also granted ACAOM's request for an expansion of scope to include candidacy reviews, thus making it possible for nonprofit, free-standing AOM institutions that have achieved candidacy status to establish eligibility for their students to participate in federal Title IV student aid programs. However, USDE's Title IV regulations require for-profit or proprietary AOM institutions to achieve accreditation to establish eligibility for their students to participate in Title IV student aid programs.

As of the summer of 2009, ACAOM had granted either full accreditation or candidate status to 62 schools at the master's level, including several branch campuses. Of these, 57 are accredited and 5 are in pre-accreditation (candidate) status. Additional AOM schools that have not achieved candidate status or accreditation with ACAOM exist in the US. As previously indicated, to date ACAOM has also approved 9 colleges to offer postgraduate clinical doctoral programs on a pilot basis, with 3 of these programs having achieved accreditation and 2 in candidacy status for this degree.

The recent national trend toward the provision of healthcare services in integrated CAM and conventional settings is reflected in the work of ACAOM's Doctoral Task Force (2003-2007), which is composed of representatives from a broad segment of the AOM profession. The task force has drafted outcomes and competency-based accreditation standards for a possible first-professional entry-level doctorate that take into account the increasing acceptance of AOM practice in conventional and complex medical environments. In a report issued in 2005, the task force recommended a list of core competencies for a possible first-professional doctorate. The task force resumed its deliberations in July of 2007 to consider accreditation standards for the doctorate, as well as related issues concerning a possible migration from the current entry-level master's degree requirement to the doctoral level. At its July meeting in 2007, the task force achieved consensus on proposed first-professional doctoral standards and competencies based on its previous report in 2005 and public comment on that report. The Commission subsequently sought public comment on the standards through an online survey and during a public hearing. In February of 2008, taking into account applicable USDE standards requiring wide acceptance of proposed standards by relevant stakeholders in order for an accrediting agency to be granted an expansion of scope for new degree levels, ACAOM determined that there is currently insufficient evidence of consensus within AOM communities of interest to justify implementation of a first-professional doctorate as entry-level into the profession. Accordingly, ACAOM urged AOM communities of interest to seek that consensus by appropriate means and indicated that the Commission would renew its efforts to develop and pilot standards for the first-professional doctorate as entry-level into the profession once that consensus is obtained.

At its Sacramento meeting in May of 2008, CCAOM adopted a formal motion in support of first-professional doctoral education in Oriental medicine and in acupuncture with appropriate standards of accreditation, stating that the CCAOM would continue to review and forward to ACAOM recommendations regarding ACAOM's draft of first-professional doctoral standards. Several CCAOM committees were charged with taking the lead on this review and CCAOM further indicated that it would initiate a dialogue toward building consensus with members of the profession concerning issues of the first-professional doctorate and its implications for the profession. In December of 2008, the American Association of Acupuncture and Oriental Medicine (AAAOM) developed and implemented a survey for the profession to determine the extent of interest in a first-professional doctorate. As of the summer of 2009, the consensus process within the profession remained uncertain but was still ongoing.

Regulation and Certification

Regulatory status

Currently, the right to practice acupuncture by comprehensively-trained, AOM practitioners exists in 44 states and in the District of Columbia. The right to practice may be designated by licensure, certification, or registration under the applicable state law. Licensure is the most common form of authorization to practice. In states without regulation, practitioners typically practice subject to potential oversight from a medical board. Other states may limit practice specifically to designated medical providers or AOM practitioners who are medically supervised. In some of the remaining unregulated states, activities to obtain full licensure status for acupuncturists are under way.

In most states with regulation, professional acupuncturists have independent status, although there remain a few states where practitioners must have supervision, prior referral, or initial diagnosis by a conventional medical doctor. The recent statutory trend, however, is in favor of more professional independence by AOM providers. The most common designation for comprehensively-trained practitioners is Licensed Acupuncturist (LAc), although in a few states they may be designated by statute as Acupuncturist Physicians (Florida) or Doctors of Oriental Medicine (New Mexico and Nevada), but these doctoral designations are licensure titles conferred by the state and do not reflect earned academic degrees at the doctoral level.

The state statutes regulating acupuncture are not uniform. In some states there are very detailed statutes and regulations, but in others there may be only a few paragraphs concerning the practice of acupuncture. The administrative structure for the regulation of acupuncture in the states also varies considerably. The most common structure is for the profession to be regulated by an independent board composed of professional acupuncturists or by a state medical board with the assistance of an advisory acupuncture board or committee. Other administrative arrangements include regulation by a joint board comprised of diverse healthcare professionals (both conventional and CAM), by the board of another CAM profession, or by a larger administrative division within a state department—all typically with the assistance of an acupuncture advisory body. This diversity reflects political and budgetary realities as each state tailors its law to meet local needs.

In general, national AOM organizations have been supportive of the adoption of state acupuncture practice acts that incorporate reference to national standards of education, training, and certification in the field. Adherence to such standards, as administered by ACAOM in the field of accreditation and by NCCAOM for certification, promotes a high level of practitioner competence and a degree of uniformity that facilitates reciprocity among the various states in the recognition of practitioner credentials.

Currently, acupuncture is not covered under the federal Loan Repayment Program. In recent years, the profession has expressed interest in and actually sought to obtain such coverage. The list of eligible providers under the Program, however, is essentially limited to those within the conventional health care field.

Examinations and certifications

Graduates of ACAOM-accredited or candidate institutions are qualified to take the national certification exams offered by the National Certification Commission for Acupuncture and Oriental

Medicine (NCCAOM). The mission of NCCAOM, which was established in 1982, is to establish, assess, and promote recognized standards of competence and safety in acupuncture and Oriental medicine for the protection and benefit of the public. The NCCAOM is a member of the National Organization for Competency Assurance (NOCA) and its programs are accredited by the National Commission for Certifying Agencies (NCCA), which represents the highest voluntary certification standards in the US. Passage of one or more of NCCAOM's national examinations is a route of licensure recognized in 43 states and the District of Columbia. Candidates who pass the Commission's certification exams in Oriental Medicine, Acupuncture with Point Location, Chinese Herbology, or Asian Bodywork Therapy are awarded the designation NCCAOM *Diplomate* appropriate to the certification achieved: Dipl. O.M. (NCCAOM), Dipl. Ac. (NCCAOM), Dipl. C.H. (NCCAOM), Dipl. ABT. (NCCAOM).

The first NCCAOM comprehensive written examination in acupuncture was administered in 1985 and was developed over a three-year period with the assistance of leading acupuncturists throughout the US. In 1989 NCCAOM added a practical examination of point location skills as a component of its acupuncture examination. A clean needle technique exam was added to the certification requirements for the acupuncture written exam in 1991 and merged into the acupuncture exam in 1998. The NCCAOM administered the first national examination in Chinese Herbology in 1995 and in 2000 offered its first written examination in Asian Bodywork Therapy. In 2003, NCCAOM began to offer an umbrella certification in Oriental Medicine to applicants who demonstrated competence in both acupuncture and Chinese herbology, as well as entry-level competency in biomedicine. Since its inception, the NCCAOM has issued more than 19,000 certificates in Acupuncture, Oriental Medicine, Chinese Herbology, and Asian Bodywork Therapy and reports the existence of more than 14,000 active Diplomates worldwide in current practice.

Research

Research in the US on the efficacy of AOM increased after 1996 when the FDA reclassified acupuncture needles from experimental devices (Class III) to devices for which performance standards exist (Class II). This provided reasonable assurance that acupuncture needles would be safe, thus making research easier to conduct. Subsequent investigations over the last decade have found that acupuncture needles had few side effects, making them somewhat safer than certain conventional western medical treatments for many diseases. Research in AOM has increased dramatically over the past decade within the US, as well as in Asia, Europe, and South America.

Among the more prominent scientific endorsements of the efficacy of acupuncture is that of the National Institutes of Health, which concluded in a 1997 Consensus Statement that:

> ...promising results have emerged, for example, showing efficacy of acupuncture in adult postoperative and chemotherapy nausea and vomiting and in postoperative dental pain. There are other situations such as addiction, stroke rehabilitation, headache, menstrual cramps, tennis elbow, fibromyalgia, myofascial pain, osteoarthritis, low back pain, carpal tunnel syndrome, and asthma, in which acupuncture may be useful as an adjunct treatment or an acceptable alternative or be included in a comprehensive management program. Further research is likely to uncover additional areas where acupuncture interventions will be useful. (NIH Consensus Statement—Acupuncture, Vol. 15, No. 5; Nov. 3-5, 1997)

Within the AOM profession, the most prominent research organization in the US is the Society for Acupuncture Research (SAR), which was formally established in 1993 and whose mission is to promote, advance, and disseminate scientific inquiry into Oriental medicine systems, which include acupuncture, herbal therapy and other modalities. SAR values quantitative and qualitative research addressing clinical efficacy, physiological mechanisms, patterns of use, and theoretical foundations. The organization sponsors annual symposia on research methodologies and welcomes individual affiliates including researchers, educators, students, acupuncturists, healthcare practitioners, and members of the public, as well as institutional affiliates including schools, vendors, and other organizations.

In November 2007, SAR held an international symposium aimed at presenting and discussing the progress made in acupuncture research during the decade following the NIH Consensus Development Conference. The symposium presentations, as well as their summaries are published in the *Journal of Alternative and Complementary Medicine* (MacPherson et al., 2008; Park et al.,

2008; Napadow et al., 2008). These reports unequivocally show that the field of acupuncture research has significantly expanded and matured since 1997. Phase II/III sham controlled trials have been successfully completed and a broad range of basic research studies have identified numerous biochemical and physiological correlates of acupuncture. However, SAR has also identified intriguing paradoxes emerging from the symposium and summaries, which are currently being explored in a white paper soon to be submitted for publication.

A survey conducted in 2005 concerning research activities at CCAOM member schools indicated that, of the 46 institutions responding to the survey, 12 were then engaged in formal AOM research activity and 13 had a research director on staff. At two other colleges where there was no research director per se, research was administered by different procedures. Research at the 12 institutions then engaged in research activity was externally funded at four colleges, internally funded at three, and funded by both means at five institutions. Some 28 colleges reported having AOM research coursework, which was required at 27 institutions and offered as an elective at 1 college. Two schools offered AOM research coursework as both a requirement and as an elective.

A sampling of research projects reported by the colleges included:

- Effectiveness of acupuncture for osteoarthritis of the knee
- Acupuncture for the treatment of stroke patients
- Acupuncture and weight reduction
- Acupuncture and herbs for the treatment of obesity
- Building a base for research activity by establishing a data collection project and tracking internal clinical outcomes
- Physiologic variability of electrical skin resistance measurements at the Ting acupuncture points
- Acupuncture for chemotherapy-induced neutropenia
- Acupuncture for adolescent endometriosis-related pain
- Development of an Oriental medicine assessment instrument
- Comparison of TCM to hormone therapy for endometriosis-related pelvic pain
- Treatment of multiple sclerosis-specific fatigue with TCM (a randomized, placebo-controlled pilot study)

- Complementary medicine approaches to TMD pain management
- Expectation and response to L-DOPA and acupuncture in Parkinson's disease
- Bioelectrical properties of acupuncture points and meridians
- Thermography on acupuncture points
- Molecular acupuncture
- AOM treatment efficacy for common pain management problems
- Assessing the quality of reporting of randomized controlled trials of acupuncture

Challenges and Opportunities

Key challenges 2009–2012

- Need for greater consensus concerning the most appropriate entry-level standard for the AOM profession (i.e., current master's or a future doctorate degree) and the content of doctoral-level course work
- Need for greater public awareness of the skill limitations of other healthcare providers who practice acupuncture without having completed a full three- or four-year AOM curriculum at an accredited AOM institution or program
- Need for greater reciprocity among states in recognizing the credentials of AOM providers
- Need for an appropriate response to increasing professional and public expectations for integrated health care
- Regulatory uncertainty concerning FDA restrictions on the use of Chinese herbs
- Need for reimbursement for AOM treatments by HMOs, Medicare, and third-party payers, and for identification of practitioner qualifications/standards for obtaining such reimbursement
- Need for greater emphasis on AOM research, training of AOM researchers, and increased funding for AOM research
- Need to strengthen and coordinate national representation and AOM profession's voice for federal policy issues
- Need for greater public awareness and acceptance of AOM with associated increase in viable professional practice

opportunities for a greater number of AOM practitioners many of whom graduate with substantial student loan debt
- Need for greater awareness of the qualifications of licensed acupuncturists in the provider credentialing process at hospitals and major medical centers
- Need for more comprehensive and coordinated collection of data concerning the profession

Key opportunities 2009–2012
- Work of ACAOM's Doctoral Task Force may produce a consensus curriculum eventually leading to a first-professional entry-level doctorate in AOM
- Increase in number of AOM schools offering postgraduate clinical education through the Doctorate of Acupuncture and Oriental Medicine and Doctorate in Acupuncture degrees
- Work of ACCAHC focusing on interdisciplinary CAM and conventional healthcare education
- Growing commitment within the profession for greater collaboration within the field, including joint projects
- Increased marketing activities to develop public awareness of the benefits, safety, and cost-effectiveness of AOM
- Success and visibility of emergency acupuncture services provided in aftermath of Hurricane Katrina may be precedent for similar opportunities in future emergency situations and for greater coordination within the profession for local emergency response
- Initial efforts underway to obtain greater recognition of acupuncture as a separate profession under the federal Standard Occupational Classification (SOC)

Resources

Organizations and websites
- Accreditation Commission for Acupuncture and Oriental Medicine (ACAOM)
  www.acaom.org
- Acupuncturists Without Borders
  www.acuwithoutborders.org
- American Association of Acupuncture and Oriental Medicine (AAAOM)
  www.aaaomonline.org

- American Organization for Bodywork Therapies of Asia (AOBTA)
  www.aobta.org
- Council of Colleges of Acupuncture and Oriental Medicine (CCAOM)
  www.ccaom.org
- Federation of Acupuncture and Oriental Medicine Regulatory Agencies (FAOMRA)
  www.faomra.com
- National Acupuncture Detoxification Association (NADA)
  www.acudetox.com
- National Acupuncture Foundation (NAF)
  www.nationalacupuncturefoundation.org
- National Certification Commission for Acupuncture and Oriental Medicine (NCCAOM)
  www.nccaom.org
- Society for Acupuncture Research (SAR)
  www.acupunctureresearch.org

Bibliography

Bensky D, Barolet R, Ellis A, Scheid V. *Chinese Herbal Medicine Formulas and Strategies*. 2nd ed. Seattle, WA: Eastland Press; 2009.

Bensky D, Clavey S, Stroger E. *Chinese Herbal Medicine Materia Medica*, 3rd ed. Seattle, WA: Eastland Press; 2004.

Chen J, Chen T. *Chinese Herbal Formulas and Applications: Pharmacological Effects and Clinical Research*. City of Industry, CA: Art of Medicine Press; 2009.

Chen J, Chen T. *Chinese Herbal Medicine and Pharmacology*. City of Industry, CA: Art of Medicine Press; 2003.

Cheng X, ed. *Chinese Acupuncture and Moxibustion*. Beijing, China: Foreign Languages Press; 1987.

Deadman P, Al-Khafaji A. *A Manual of Acupuncture*. Sussex, England: Journal of Chinese Medicine Publications; 1998.

Huang Ti Nei Ching Su Wen. Veith I, trans. Berkeley, CA: University of California Press; 1949.

Maciocia G. *The Foundations of Chinese Medicine*. Philadelphia, PA: Churchill Livingstone; 1989.

Nan Ching. Unschuld P, trans. Berkeley, CA: University of California Press; 1986.

Unschuld P. *Huang Di Nei Jing Su Wen: Nature, Knowledge, Imagery in an Ancient Chinese Medical Text*. Berkeley, CA: University of California Press; 2003.

Unschuld P. *Medicine in China: A History of Ideas*. Berkeley, CA: University of California Press; 1988.

Wiseman N, Ye F. *A Practical Dictionary of Chinese Medicine*. Brookline, MA: Paradigm Publications; 1998.

Zmiewski P, Wiseman N, Ellis A, eds. *Fundamentals of Chinese Medicine*. Brookline, MA: Paradigm Publications; 1985.

Chiropractic

Reed Phillips, DC, PhD, Michael Wiles, DC, MEd, David O'Bryon, JD, CAE

Partner Organization: Association of Chiropractic Colleges

About the Authors: Phillips is immediate past president of the Southern California University of Health Sciences, past vice president with the Foundation for Chiropractic Education and Research, a past president of the Association of Chiropractic Colleges (ACC), of The Council on Chiropractic Education, of The Councils on Chiropractic Education International, and founding chair of ACCAHC. Wiles is provost and vice president for academic affairs of Northwestern Health Sciences University and co-chair of the ACCAHC Education Working Group. O'Bryon is executive director of the ACC, vice chair of ACCAHC, and immediate past president of the Federation of Associations of Schools of the Allied Health Professions.

Philosophy, Mission, Goals

Chiropractic is a healthcare discipline that emphasizes the inherent power of the body to heal itself without the use of drugs or surgery. It focuses on the relationship between the body's structure (primarily the spine) and function (as coordinated by the nervous system) and how that relationship affects the preservation and restoration of health.[1]

The above statement is taken from a definition provided by the Association of Chiropractic Colleges and is generally accepted by institutions offering chiropractic degree programs. Preferences and practices vary, however, about the way the profession describes itself. A graduate of a program may prefer any of a range of titles: chiropractor, doctor of chiropractic, doctor of chiropractic medicine, or chiropractic physician. Some will only use "chiropractic" to describe the practice while others prefer "chiropractic medicine."

This range of usages is also found in regulatory and self-regulatory agencies. In some jurisdictions, state law limits the terms

---

[1] www.chirocolleges.org Web page for the Association of Chiropractic Colleges, see "chiropractic paradigm."

that may or may not be used. The most recent Department of Labor description includes the terms chiropractic physician and chiropractic medicine, language also used by the Council on Chiropractic Education, the US Department of Education-recognized accreditation agency. Inside the Association of Chiropractic Colleges, individual school members also choose different language.

For this reason, we will, in this chapter, intersperse mixed use of these terms. We urge practitioners from other disciplines to engage the members of the chiropractic profession on their preferences. This may provide a useful way to improve understanding and collaboration.

Early chiropractic concepts of heath and disease were compatible with vitalistic philosophies of the late 19th century. Living cells were conceived as having an inborn intelligent component that was responsible for the maintenance of life. This phenomenon is analogous to homeostasis. Homeostatic control mechanisms function largely as a result of coordination of sensory input and motor output through the central nervous system. The intimacy of body structure (particularly the spine) and the nervous system, and hence body function, led the early chiropractors to develop a philosophy of care that, in essence, posited that a normally functioning nervous system, in the presence of structural normality, should lead to normal health. This vitalistic approach toward health and disease was similar to that proposed by the early osteopathic profession.

The Council on Chiropractic Education states: "A doctor of chiropractic is a primary care physician whose purpose, as a practitioner of the healing arts, is to help meet the health needs of individual patients and of the public, giving particular attention to the structural and neurological aspects of the body… As a gatekeeper for direct access to the health delivery system, the doctor of chiropractic's responsibilities as a primary care physician include wellness promotion, health assessment, diagnosis and the chiropractic management of the patient's health care needs. When indicated, the doctor of chiropractic consults with, co-manages, or refers to other health care providers."

History of the profession

Chiropractic was founded by Daniel David Palmer in Davenport, Iowa, in 1895. Palmer was originally a schoolteacher who developed an interest in magnetism and what was popularly called magnetic healing at that time. Having observed that a patient's deafness had apparently occurred following a traumatic experience resulting in a protuberance on his spine, Palmer reasoned that reduction of this protuberance might affect the patient's hearing. Evidently, following a manipulation of the spine, the patient's hearing improved. This led to the formulation of a theory relating spinal alignment to states of health and disease which was similar to that espoused by Andrew Taylor Still, the founder of osteopathy, in 1874 in neighboring Missouri.

In 1975, the National Institutes of Health sponsored an interdisciplinary conference called "The Research Status of Spinal Manipulative Therapy" in Bethesda, Maryland. This conference brought together leaders in the field of spinal manipulation from the chiropractic, medical, and osteopathic professions from around the world. It marked a significant point in the evolution of chiropractic education and practice, and important progress has been made since that time toward the integration of chiropractic education, science, research, and practice into mainstream systems of health care and professional education. While this process is far from complete, the chiropractic profession of today can be proud of the great advances in education and research of the past few decades.

Chiropractic spread first to Canada, then to the United Kingdom, and finally throughout the world from these simple roots in Davenport, Iowa. In fact, the World Heath Organization has published guidelines recommending minimum educational standards for the regulation of chiropractic services in national healthcare systems.

Characteristics and Data

The chiropractic medical profession is growing rapidly throughout the world. There are approximately 60,000 chiropractors in the US and about another 15,000 in the rest of the world. Doctors of chiropractic are regulated as a licensed health profession in all 50 US states, all 10 Canadian provinces, in Mexico, and in about 40 other countries. In roughly 60 other countries, chiropractors practice in an unregulated fashion, although there is a constant movement toward officially regulating the practice of chiropractic in these countries. In the countries where chiropractic medicine is regulated, most of the chiropractic colleges are located within university settings. The International Council on Chiropractic Education and the International

Board of Chiropractic Examiners are working with the as yet unregulated countries to maintain a standard of education and examination that can be accepted worldwide.

Income data vary for chiropractors, depending on the country
and source of the data. Most sources suggest that full-time chiropractic physicians earn an income comparable with other health
professionals, with recent surveys setting the average income in the
$90,000–$110,000 range.

Clinical Care

Approach to patient care

Today, the vitalistic philosophy survives in the form of an approach to patient care that recognizes and honors the body's own
innate mechanisms for adaptation and homeostasis. Treatment is
therefore designed to accommodate those mechanisms as much as
possible.

In practical terms, this can be translated into an approach to
care that seeks to relieve symptoms, restore as much structural normality as possible (particularly for the spine and axial skeleton),
and support and strengthen body structure so that it results in optimal body function. A patient may seek help for lower back pain,
for example, and this approach to care will address not only the
local factors associated with the back pain, but also the structural
adaptations that may have led to it in the first place, such as weak
abdominal muscles, obesity, stressful work postures, and other factors. Such an approach can be considered both patient-centered
and holistic.

The general approach of doctors of chiropractic to patient care
is similar to that of conventional medical doctors. That is, the patient is interviewed and examined, following which a diagnosis is
formulated and a treatment plan constructed. Treatment progress
is monitored by reassessment, and the patient is discharged from
care when the appropriate outcomes have been achieved.

More specifically, chiropractic physicians obtain a standard
medical history. They are particularly concerned with the identification of factors or conditions requiring either referral to, or co-
treatment with, other providers. The examination of the patient
is likewise similar to that performed by other physicians and includes the typical components of a general physical examination.
Doctors of chiropractic, like other physicians, may perform a lim-

ited or focused examination according to the nature of the patient's chief complaint. Chiropractors emphasize the examination of the musculoskeletal system but include all necessary examination procedures to arrive at a diagnosis. Most chiropractic patients present with complaints related to the musculoskeletal system; accordingly, musculoskeletal diagnoses are most common in chiropractic practice. Doctors of chiropractic focus on the structural component of a patient's complaint and, where possible, relate the patient's complaint to local and general structural factors. For example, a lower back complaint may be related locally to a sacro-iliac joint dysfunction, but generally to poor posture and obesity, all of which must be taken into consideration in the comprehensive treatment plan.

Treatment plans are developed to provide symptom relief and achieve problem resolution. Typically, treatment involves some form of manual therapy, most often including spinal manipulation, but other forms of treatment are also very commonly used. These include, but are not limited to, exercise, physical therapeutics (such as electrotherapy, hydrotherapy, or ultrasound, for example), nutritional counseling, lifestyle advice, and counseling.

Manual therapy includes a continuum of treatment methods ranging from very gentle and low-force techniques, up to specific high-velocity, low-amplitude chiropractic adjustments. Some techniques are mechanically assisted using articulated treatment tables, and some techniques use a mechanical device to introduce a small mechanical force into the tissues. There is a very wide spectrum of techniques and methods under the umbrella of manual therapies, but the one most commonly associated with chiropractic treatment is the chiropractic adjustment (typically a high-velocity, low-amplitude thrust).

The therapeutic target of the chiropractic adjustment is the mechanical phenomenon known to chiropractors as subluxation—in more modern terms, a functional articular lesion. This lesion represents a correctible segmental neuro-mechanical phenomenon associated with asymmetry, restriction of motion, and palpable tissue texture abnormalities and tenderness. Neurologically, it has been associated with spinal segmental facilitation and occasionally with trophic changes. This "manipulable lesion," as some have called it, is widely known to practitioners of manual medicine and spinal manipulation but is not generally known or appreciated outside of those fields. Early chiropractic concepts of a "bone out of place, pinching a nerve" have dogged the profession for decades and hindered inter-professional dialogue with regard to this lesion and phenomenon. A new generation of chiropractors and chiropractic educators are making strides towards standardization of terminology, the elucidation of the properties of this lesion, and the biomechanical effects of spinal manipulative therapy.

The majority of patients consult a chiropractor for complaints directly related to back pain (about 60%) while other musculoskeletal complaints account for another 20% of new patient consultations. Headaches (10%) and non-musculoskeletal conditions that appear to respond to manipulative therapy or have a structural component (10%) account for the remainder of patients seen in chiropractic practice.

Scope of practice

The scope of practice for doctors of chiropractic may differ somewhat depending on the location or jurisdiction, just as do the acceptable terms, such as chiropractor, chiropractic physician, or doctor of chiropractic. Generally speaking, there are three common features of legislation and practice in all jurisdictions:

- primary contact practice, in which doctors of chiropractic are legally permitted to have direct contact with new patients without the necessity of referral
- the right and obligation to make a diagnosis of a patient prior to the initiation of treatment, including performing or ordering diagnostic imaging studies
- the prohibition of the use of prescription drugs or surgery. Some jurisdictions allow minor surgery or even the practice of obstetrics, but chiropractors do not typically perform surgery or prescribe drugs.

The wording of the scope of practice in legislation shaping chiropractic medicine varies widely, but in general it includes the diagnosis, treatment, and prevention of musculoskeletal disorders using manual treatment methods, and the use of adjunctive approaches such as nutritional therapy, counseling, and physical therapeutics, without the use of drugs or surgery.

Referral practices

Chiropractic students are taught the importance of proper and appropriate referral to other providers. Chiropractic medical education emphasizes the identification of conditions not amenable to chiropractic care and the process of referring such patients to those who can properly care for them. Since back pain can be due to serious diseases and conditions, some of which require urgent referral (such as cauda equina syndrome), doctors of chiropractic are always alert to the possibility of such conditions. Generally speaking, practicing chiropractic physicians seek to develop referral relationships with conventional medical, osteopathic, or naturopathic family physicians, orthopedic surgeons, rheumatologists, neurologists, and gynecologists. Obviously, the needs of their patients may also require referral to other specialists, including massage therapists, acupuncturists, or other complementary and alternative healthcare practitioners, but the above list is representative of the needs of most chiropractors.

Many chiropractors will also choose to develop a referral network and relationship with other chiropractic physicians, particularly those specializing in certain conditions, and also with physical therapists. While the training and methods for chiropractors and physical therapists overlap to a certain degree, there are differences in their approaches to patient care and in the specific nature of their practices.

Doctors of chiropractic also appreciate and seek the referral of patients from other providers. Specifically, they welcome patients with complaints referable to the musculoskeletal system, such as back pain, neck pain, mechanical headaches, sports injuries, repetitive strain injuries, motor vehicle accident injuries, work-related musculoskeletal injuries, overuse syndromes, and other similar conditions. Chiropractors are happy to set up mutual referral networks with other physicians and other healthcare providers. Typically, the various providers will meet to become familiar with each other's practices and eventually develop a complementary referral practice. Chiropractic physicians are trained to provide a referral consultation note summarizing their findings and proposed care.

Third-party payers

Insurance coverage and third-party payment for chiropractic medical services vary widely from jurisdiction to jurisdiction. Chiropractic medicine is widely covered through private insurance plans in most countries, particularly in the US. Most government sponsored workers' compensation plans cover chiropractic services at some level. There is an increasing tendency for chiropractic medicine to be included in wellness programs or other similar employer-sponsored health plans.

Integration Activities

All educational institutions offering chiropractic education have student clinics where the underserved or uninsured may receive chiropractic care at little or no cost. A growing number of community clinics include chiropractic medical services alongside the services of medical doctors and other healthcare services. Chiropractic physicians are increasingly involved in larger clinics and hospitals, and a growing number of hospitals grant limited privileges to chiropractors to treat patients on an outpatient basis or to use diagnostic facilities.

There are many other clinical settings where doctors of chiropractic are part of a multidisciplinary team. An outstanding example is the doctor of chiropractic who serves in the Bethesda Naval Hospital. His presence there is the outcome of ongoing negotiations with the US Department of Defense to employ doctors of chiropractic in military healthcare facilities as directed by Congress and the President of the United States.

Following recent legislation, chiropractic medicine is gradually becoming available throughout the military healthcare system. Experience to date has shown that chiropractic physicians in military heathcare facilities quickly become integral and valued members of the healthcare team.

With Presidential insistence, chiropractic medicine has also been introduced into the US Veterans Administration healthcare system. A three-year dialogue with a Federal Advisory Committee consisting of medical and osteopathic physicians, a physical therapist, a physician's assistant, and several doctors of chiropractic resulted in a list of 68 recommendations to the Secretary of the Veteran's Administration on the implementation process. Of the 68 recommendations, 67 were unanimously agreed upon. This program is slowly expanding throughout the entire VA system and current laws mandate the inclusion of chiropractic medical services at all VA facilities within the next few years. Several chiropractic educational institutions now have agreements with their local VA hospitals, allowing clinical rotations of senior chiropractic students and interns, and facilitating interaction of conventional medical and chiropractic students, interns, and residents.

Chiropractic has become a highly accepted form of treatment in the world of sports. Most major professional teams in all sports have a team chiropractic physician. Many college and university teams engage the services of a doctor of chiropractic as well. Doctors of chiropractic provide care in many international events in wrestling, track and field, swimming, and other sports, and are increasingly participating on multidisciplinary healthcare teams at the Olympics and in professional sports. For example, a chiropractor is on staff at the US Olympic Training Center in Colorado Springs, Colorado.

As the world of complementary and alternative health care continues to grow and gain public acceptance, doctors of chiropractic medicine are at the forefront in many areas and are providing leadership to help the entire CAM community establish standards and achieve cultural recognition. Several chiropractic educational institutions have incorporated programs in acupuncture and Oriental medicine within their structure, at least one has added a program in naturopathic medicine, and many teach the principles and application of homeopathic formularies, clinical nutrition, yoga, and massage therapy.

Over the last decade of increased integration activity, individual doctors of chiropractic and leaders of chiropractic programs have engaged various inter-professional and inter-institutional relationships with integrative medical programs that are among the 45 member programs of the Consortium of Academic Health Centers for Integrative Medicine. Among these are programs at Yale University, Harvard University, the University of Minnesota, and Oregon Health and Sciences University (OHSU). In the latter instance, the president of Western States Chiropractic College has a board position on the Oregon Collaborative for Integrative Medicine, where his colleagues include academic leaders at OHSU as well as the presidents of an acupuncture and Oriental medical college and a naturopathic medical school that are also located in Portland, Oregon. The direction of growth and development is toward a more integrated practice among all the disciplines.

Education

Schools and programs
Chiropractic colleges in the US grant the Doctor of Chiropractic degree after a course of study which is generally a minimum of

about 4200 hours, typically over a 4–5 year academic year program. There are 17 educational institutions in the US and two in Canada that offer chiropractic doctorates. These include individual chiropractic colleges, colleges within a private university, and colleges within a public university system. Typically, chiropractic students are in their mid-twenties, with about 75% having completed undergraduate degrees before entering chiropractic college.

At least 90 semester hours (three years) in undergraduate studies in the biological, physical, and social sciences are required prior to admission to chiropractic medical programs in the US. Outside the US, many programs begin after secondary school at the collegiate level and are five years in length. In those instances, the requisite basic science courses typically are included in the first two years of five-year programs.

After completing the program of studies, the successful student graduates with a Doctor of Chiropractic (DC) degree in the US. Outside of the US, graduates of chiropractic programs may receive a variety of degrees and designations. The most common are Bachelor of Science and Master of Science degrees in Chiropractic, and a Bachelor of Chiropractic (BChir), somewhat analogous in the UK to a Bachelor of Medicine (MB or BMed) degree.

The Association of Chiropractic Colleges (ACC) represents all accredited colleges in the US and several others from around the world. Programs outside the US are usually affiliated with public universities. Programs exist in Canada (2), Mexico (2), Brazil (2), Spain (2), UK (2), Denmark (1), Switzerland (1), Sweden (1), South Africa (2), Australia (3), New Zealand (1), and Japan (1). Additional programs are under development in Argentina (and possibly Chile), Norway, Japan, and several other countries.

Curriculum content

The chiropractic curriculum typically includes (but is not limited to) courses in:

- Anatomy
- Biochemistry
- Physiology
- Microbiology and Immunology
- Pathology
- Public Health

- Clinical Skills (including history and physical examination)
- Clinical and Laboratory Diagnosis
- Clinical Sciences (including the study of cardiopulmonary, gastrointestinal, and genitourinary disorders; dermatology; ophthalmology; otolaryngology)
- Gynecology and Obstetrics
- Pediatrics
- Geriatrics
- Diagnostic Imaging (procedures and interpretation)
- Psychology and Abnormal Psychology
- Nutrition and Clinical Nutrition
- Biomechanics
- Orthopedics
- Neurology
- Emergency Procedures and First-Aid
- Spinal Analysis
- Principles and Practice of Chiropractic
- Clinical Reasoning and Decision Making
- Chiropractic Manual Therapy and Adjustive Procedures
- Research Methods and Statistics
- Professional Practice Ethics and Office Management

There are many opportunities for postgraduate study in chiropractic. A number of full-time residency programs exist, of which the most popular and ubiquitous is diagnostic imaging (a three-year, full-time residency). A full-time residency program in chiropractic geriatrics was recently initiated at Northwestern Health Sciences University, and National University of Health Sciences offers three-year residency programs in family practice and research. Other institutions are offering additional degree programs. Numerous certification programs exist in a variety of subject areas such as orthopedics, pediatrics, sports injuries, and nutrition, and are typically taught at chiropractic colleges or through professional associations. Finally, there are growing numbers of accredited programs offering master's degrees in chiropractic specialties, which are completed following either part-time (including hybrid and online learning) or full-time residential programs at institutions that offer chiropractic degree programs. Examples are master of science degrees in applied clinical nutrition at New York Chiropractic College, in health promotion at Cleveland Chiropractic

College, and in sports science and rehabilitation at Logan College of Chiropractic.

Accreditation

Each college in the United States that is a member of the ACC is accredited by the Council on Chiropractic Education (www. cce-usa.org). The Council on Chiropractic Education (CCE) is the agency recognized by the US Secretary of Education for accreditation of programs and institutions offering the Doctor of Chiropractic degree. CCE ensures the quality of chiropractic medical education in the US by means of accreditation, educational improvement, and public information. CCE develops accreditation criteria to assess how effectively programs or institutions plan, implement and evaluate their mission and goals, program objectives, inputs, resources, and outcomes of their chiropractic programs.

The CCE is also recognized by the Council for Higher Education Accreditation (CHEA) and the Association of Specialized and Professional Accreditors (ASPA).[2] All but two of the institutions with chiropractic programs in the US also maintain institutional accreditation through their regional post-secondary accrediting associations.

National accrediting bodies are also located in Canada (www. chirofed.ca), Europe (www.cce-europe.org), and Australasia (www. ccea.com.au). Together, these accrediting bodies form the Council on Chiropractic Education International (CCEI) (www.cceintl.org). CCEI is committed to excellence in chiropractic education through its *Model Core Chiropractic Educational Standards* and through aid in the development and recognition of new accrediting bodies in geographic regions where such agencies are not currently recognized. CCEI provides accreditation services through its assigned member organizations to chiropractic educational entities situated in areas not currently served by a CCEI member agency. Accreditation agency actions and status designations for chiropractic educational entities that award equivalent degrees are mutually endorsed on the basis of membership in CCEI. CCEI has established the following goals:

1. Define minimal model educational standards and ensure their adoption and maintenance by accrediting agencies worldwide;

---

[2] www.cce-usa.org Web page for the Council on Chiropractic Education in the United States.

2. Define the process of accreditation and assure appropriate implementation and administration of the process by accrediting agencies worldwide;
3. Establish and maintain a process for verifying the equivalence of the educational standards and accreditation process utilized by CCEI member accrediting organizations worldwide;
4. Assist and provide guidance for the development of accrediting agencies toward their full autonomy and membership in CCEI;
5. Promote a continuous model of educational standards, recognizing educational, cultural and legislative diversity in various countries and regions; and
6. Advocate quality education through the dissemination and promotion of information to governments, professional organizations, and others.[3]

Regulation and Certification

Regulatory status
Doctors of Chiropractic are regulated in all fifty states and the US territories. Licensing boards from each state are members of the Federation of Chiropractic Licensing Boards (FCLB) (www.fclb.org). The FCLB mission statement is "To protect the public and to serve our member boards by promoting excellence in chiropractic regulation."[3]

Licensing laws differ between the various states, although the underlying commonality is generally related to diagnosis of spinal and articular dysfunction and its correction, mostly by the use of spinal manipulation and manual therapies. Some states such as Oregon, Illinois, Oklahoma, and New Mexico allow a broader scope of practice, while some states such as Washington and Michigan are noted for their very restrictive scope of practice. (Efforts are under way in both of these states to expand the scope.) Most members of state licensing boards are governmental appointees and serve limited terms. Most boards also have non-clinical members serving with clinical members. For more information on scope of practice go to www.fclb.org/directory/index.html. The FCLB also maintains a listing of actions taken against individual chiropractors in

[3] www.fclb.org Web page for the Federation of Chiropractic Licensing Boards.

their Chiropractic Information Network-Board Action Databank (CIN-BAD), accessible on their web page for a fee.

Similar organizations operate in Canada, Europe, and Australia. Local jurisdiction regulations also vary in each of these countries. Chiropractic medicine is also practiced in many countries where official legal recognition has not yet occurred; in unregulated locations, those claiming to practice chiropractic often come from very diverse backgrounds and may lack any formal education or training beyond a few seminars. The World Federation of Chiropractic (www.wfc.org) has been operational for 20 years and has had significant influence and success in promoting legislation and standards for chiropractic practice.

Examinations and certifications

The National Board of Chiropractic Examiners (NBCE) is the principal testing agency for the chiropractic profession. Established in 1963, the NBCE develops and administers standardized national examinations according to established guidelines. NBCE is dedicated to promoting excellence in the chiropractic profession by providing testing programs that measure educational attainment and clinical competency of those seeking licensure. Their examinations serve the needs of state licensing authorities, chiropractic colleges, educators and students, doctors of chiropractic, and the public. These examinations serve the profession and public by:

- promoting high standards of competence
- assisting state licensing agencies in assessing competence
- facilitating the licensure of newly graduated chiropractors
- enhancing professional credibility

In providing standardized written and performance assessments for the chiropractic profession, the NBCE develops, administers, analyzes, scores, and reports results from various examinations. The NBCE scores are among the criteria utilized by state licensing agencies to determine whether applicants demonstrate competency and satisfy state qualifications for licensure.

In its expanding role as an international testing agency, the NBCE espouses no particular chiropractic philosophy, but formulates test plans according to information provided collectively by the chiropractic colleges, the state licensing agencies, field practitioners, subject specialists, and a *Job Analysis of Chiropractic*.[4]

There are four national exams students take in order to apply for licensure (most states accept the National Board of Chiropractic Examiners as their basic examination for licensure). The Part IV Exam is a practical clinical exam designed to test for competency and has gained international attention from other disciplines.[5]

Recently, an International Board of Chiropractic Examiners has formed for the purpose of standardizing the formal testing of chiropractic candidates for licensure outside the US.

Research

For 60 years after its founding in 1946, the Foundation for Chiropractic Education and Research (FCER) (www.fcer.org) was the central focus of research in the profession. With the significant growth of research capacity in the chiropractic medical schools and the increasing availability of government grants, the center of research action in chiropractic medicine has shifted to these academic centers. Researchers on chiropractic with Palmer Chiropractic College, Western States Chiropractic College, Northwestern Health Sciences University, Southern California University of Health Sciences, National University of Health Sciences, and New York Chiropractic College are among those in the United States who have received significant federal grants.

The most significant effort to date has been through the Palmer Chiropractic College, which has run an NIH consortium center program for the last ten years. Palmer has also been at the center of organizing the chiropractic profession's Research Agenda Conference (RAC). This meeting has been partially supported with federal grants. The Association of Chiropractic Colleges sponsors annual conferences in which educators from around the world meet and present research papers and posters. Since the 1990s, this annual meeting has been combined with the RAC. These combined ACC-RAC conferences are attended by the academic and research community of chiropractic, as well as by basic scientists and researchers from related medical and health professions.

---

[4] National Board of Chiropractic Examiners, *The 2005 Job Analysis*. Published by the NBCE, Greeley, Colorado, 2005.

[5] www.nbce.org Web page for the National Board of Chiropractic Examiners.

A significant portion of industry support for the profession has also been funneled into research, including over $10 million from the National Chiropractic Mutual Insurance Company (NCMIC). Funds from Foot Levelers Inc. supported numerous fellowships, helping doctors of chiropractic obtain graduate research training at the master's and PhD levels. Over the past 40 years, more than 100 individual doctors of chiropractic have been trained and received either a master's degree or a PhD degree in an academic discipline at a major university through such fellowships.

The World Federation of Chiropractic (WFC) has played an important role in sponsoring biennial international research symposia for the last ten years, both in the US and internationally. These have provided a venue for research and educational specialists on an international level to present their work. The WFC is the primary organizational entity that provides a forum for dialogue and exchange on a world-wide basis. Nearing its 25th anniversary, the WFC has been productive in establishing common ground for the profession in individual countries as well as with the World Health Organization.

At the federal level in the US, within the structure of the National Institutes of Health (NIH), the formation of what started as the Office for Alternative Medicine has now grown to become the National Center for Complementary and Alternative Medicine (NCCAM). The change from having no presence at the NIH, to the formation of an Office with a budget of $2 million, to the formation of a Center with a budget in excess of $100 million is indeed evidence of dramatic growth. While the chiropractic profession does not claim sole responsibility for this growth and recognition of complementary and alternative medicine, it has nonetheless played a significant role through its research, educational, and legislative initiatives. The first member of a complementary and alternative medical profession to be hired as program officer by the NIH was a chiropractor.

Scientific journals

The Association of Chiropractic Colleges publishes the peer-reviewed *Journal of Chiropractic Education*, which is indexed in PubMed. National University of Health Sciences (NUHS) through Elsevier Publishing, supports the publication of three peer-reviewed and indexed journals: *Journal of Manipulative and Physiological Therapeutics* (JMPT), *Journal of Chiropractic Medicine* (JCM), and an online journal, *Journal of Chiropractic Humanities* (JCH). NUHS has published JMPT since 1978.

Challenges and Opportunities

Key challenges 2009–2014
- Further expansion in federal healthcare delivery systems/healthcare reform and VA internship agreements with all chiropractic colleges
- Increasing enrollment at chiropractic educational institutions
- Funding research programs, residencies, and fellowships at all chiropractic institutions
- Keeping the cost of education down
- Increasing revenue for doctors in practice
- Increasing opportunities for more integration and collaboration
- Enhancing the public image of the profession
- Achieving political unity within the profession
- Adapting the practice of chiropractic to the realities of practicing evidence-based care in a new health care reform environment, where cost, outcomes, and accountability will be key

Key opportunities 2009–2014
- Changes to our healthcare delivery system and the inclusion and integration of chiropractic medical services on a broader scale
- Continued growth and acceptance of alternative health care by the public
- Ongoing and increased research support through federal agencies such as NIH
- Continued development of chiropractic education and integration within larger university systems
- More collaborative work between the CAM professions
- Continued growth and expansion of the profession on a worldwide basis

Resources

Organizations and websites
In the US, there are two national organizations representing chiropractors: the American Chiropractic Association and the International Chiropractors Association. The World Federation of Chiropractic represents the profession on a global basis. There are approximately 75,000 chiropractic practitioners worldwide.

- American Chiropractic Association
  www.acatoday.org
- Association of Chiropractic Colleges
  www.chirocolleges.org
- Council on Chiropractic Education
  www.cce-usa.org
- Councils on Chiropractic Education International
  www.cceintl.org
- Federation of Chiropractic Licensing Boards
  www.fclb.org
- International Chiropractors Association
  www.chiropractic.org
- National Board of Chiropractic Examiners
  www.nbce.org
- World Federation of Chiropractic
  www.wfc.org

Bibliography
Christensen MG, Kollasch MW. *Job Analysis of Chiropractic 2005*. Greeley, CO: National Board of Chiropractic Examiners; 2005.

Haldeman S, ed in chief. *Principles and Practice of Chiropractic*. 2nd ed. New York, NY: McGraw-Hill; 2004.

Leach RA. *The Chiropractic Theories: A Textbook of Scientific Research*. 4th ed. Baltimore, MD: Lippincott Williams & Wilkins; 2004.

Peterson DH, Bergmann TF. *Chiropractic Technique*. 2nd ed. St. Louis, MO: Mosby; 2000.

Phillips RB. The chiropractic paradigm. *J Chiropr Educ*. 2001;15(2):49-52.

Massage Therapy

Jan Schwartz, MA, Cherie Monterastelli, RN, MS, LMT

Partner Organization:
American Massage Therapy Association—Council of Schools

About the Authors: Schwartz is past chair of the Commission on Massage Therapy Accreditation, co-owner of Education and Training Solutions, LLC, a board member of ACCAHC and co-chair of the ACCAHC Education Working Group. Monterastelli is a board member of the AMTA-COS and an ACCAHC board member.

Philosophy, Mission, Goals

Several organizations and scholars have created definitions that incorporate the mission and philosophy of massage therapy. For example, in the frequently used textbook, *Tappan's Handbook of Healing Massage Techniques*, the definition is: "Massage is the intentional and systematic manipulation of the soft tissues of the body to enhance health and healing." (Benjamin & Tappan, p. 4) Similarly, according to the American Massage Therapy Association *Glossary of Terms*, massage therapy is "a profession…with the intention of positively affecting the health and well-being of the client through a variety of touch techniques."

Because most definitions of massage therapy include the use of touch, which is a basic, non-technological approach to health and healing, it follows that most massage therapists subscribe to a natural healing philosophy. That philosophy encompasses a preference for "natural methods of healing, the belief in an innate healing force, and a holistic view of human life." (Benjamin & Tappan, p.14)

Massage therapy is an evolving profession that has grown at an extraordinary rate over the last 16 years due to consumer interest and acceptance. As a result of this rapid growth, there has been some awkwardness in the response of the profession to issues like self-definition, education, and teacher training. During this period, the number of schools expanded greatly. The pace of growth was originally set by schools owned and operated by veterans in the field, and subsequently by some corporations, community colleges, and others with limited experience with massage therapy. As a result, the profession of massage therapy does not currently have a single definition of massage. Individual states regulate massage therapy by setting legal definitions of massage and massage therapists. In many cases, states also set some form of curriculum standards for massage schools.

History of the profession

Massage is a healing modality that has been practiced by most cultures in most eras. Traditional peoples used a variety of techniques that are now known as massage, all of which included some form of person-to-person touching with the intention of manipulating and relaxing the muscles of the body. From the South Sea Islands to the Mexican peninsula and the indigenous cultures of the Americas to the ancient civilizations of Greece, Asia and Africa, historians and researchers can find evidence of the practice of massage. In India, the ancient practice of Ayurveda included forms of movement therapy and massage. In ancient Greece, Hippocrates wrote about the ability of massage to build muscle as well as heal it. China and Japan each developed varieties of natural healing that included touch and the healing force.

The more modern practice of massage, known as Western massage or Swedish massage, became prominent in the 19th and early 20th centuries. Called the father of Swedish massage, Per Henrik Ling (1776-1839) developed a series of exercises that became known as "medical gymnastics" and used a series of movements that applied resistance to the joints. These techniques, however, have little resemblance to massage as it is known today. While there was a hands-on relationship between therapist and subject, the activities were more like those used by physical therapists than massage therapists. Ling's perspective on the practices he was developing evolved, however, and he began to consider the relationship between the physical and mental aspects of wellness, the mind/body connection, which is today very much a part of Swedish massage and other massage modalities.

Not quite a century later, a Dutch physician named Johann Georg Mezger (1838-1909) developed the techniques that are now the basis for Swedish massage:

- Effleurage: Long, gliding strokes
- Petrissage: Lifting and kneading the muscles
- Friction: Firm, deep, circular rubbing movements
- Tapotement: Brisk tapping or percussive movements
- Vibration: Rapidly shaking or vibrating specific muscles

Researchers noticed the similarities between the work of Ling and Mezger and gave Sweden the credit for developing these techniques.

Characteristics and Data[1]

Industry research estimates that there are 280,000–320,000 practicing massage therapists and massage school students in the US. Today's massage therapists are likely to enter the massage therapy profession as a second career and are predominantly female (88%). Although there are a number of younger and older massage therapists currently practicing, the average age of a practitioner is the mid-40s. They are also most likely to be sole practitioners.

Massage therapists earn a comparable annual income to other healthcare support workers, according to the US Department of Labor Statistics. In 2008, the average annual income for a massage therapist who provides 15 hours of massage per week was $31,500. More than half of massage therapists (58%) also earned income working in another profession. The average time working in the industry was 6.3 years.

Sole practitioners represent the majority of massage therapists; however, there has been an increase in the number of massage therapists directly employed by spas, working in healthcare settings or as contractors. Most work an average of 19 hours a week providing massage and give an average of 41 massages per month.

Growth in the healthcare industry is providing numerous jobs for massage therapists. From 2005 to 2006, the percentage of massage therapists who worked in a healthcare environment increased from 10% to 13%. According to a 2005 survey on complementary and alternative medicine (CAM) conducted for the American Hospital Association, nearly 27% of the hospitals that responded offered one or more CAM therapies. Massage therapy was the top CAM therapy provided for both inpatients and outpatients.

---

[1] Data from the American Massage Therapy Association website. Detailed information available at http://www.amtamassage.org/news/MTIndustryFactSheet.html.

According to the Associated Bodywork & Massage Profession-al's 2009 survey results there were 1,568 state-approved massage therapy programs in the US. Of those schools/programs, less than half are accredited. Between 2001 and 2008, the massage therapy profession experienced over 70% growth in the school market. The reason for this growth is the rapid consumer acceptance of massage therapy. It should be noted that there is an extraordinarily high ra-tio of positive to negative experiences with massage.

Clinical Care

Approach to patient care

Massage therapists use their expertise in a variety of modali-ties. Definitions of modalities from the glossary of terms provided by Associated Bodywork & Massage Professionals (ABMP) and the American Massage Therapy Association (AMTA) include:

- **Onsite Massage** (also known as chair massage or seated massage)—Is administered while the client is clothed and seated in a specially designed chair. Onsite massage usually lasts between 15 and 30 minutes and is intended to relax and improve circulation.
- **Western Massage**—One of the most commonly taught and well-known massage techniques, Western massage is a form of soft tissue manipulation. The technique categories com-monly used to describe Western massage are effleurage, petrissage, tapotement, friction, vibration, touch without movement, and joint movement.
- **Deep Tissue**—A general term for a range of therapies that seeks to improve the function of the body's connective tis-sues and/or muscles; deep tissue work releases the chronic patterns of tension in the body through slow strokes and deep finger pressure on the muscles, tendons, and fascia. These techniques require advanced training and a thorough understanding of anatomy and physiology.
- **Myofascial Release**—A hands-on technique that provides sustained pressure into myofascial restrictions to eliminate pain and restore motion. The theory of myofascial release re-quires an understanding of the fascial system (or connective tissue). The fascia is a specialized system of the body that

has been compared to a tensegrity model, which is woven throughout the body; localized fascial restrictions may cause problems in remote areas of the body.

- **Trigger Point Therapy**—Based on the discoveries of Janet Travell, MD and David Simons, MD, in which they found the causal relationship between chronic pain and its source, myofascial trigger point therapy is used to relieve muscular pain and dysfunction through applied pressure to trigger points of referred pain and through stretching exercises. These points are defined as localized areas in which the muscles and connective tissues are highly sensitive to pain when compressed. Pressure on these points can send referred pain to other parts of the body.
- **Sports Massage**—Massage therapy focusing on muscle systems relevant to a particular sport and designed to enhance athletic performance and recovery. The three contexts in which sports massage can be useful to an athlete are pre-event, post-event, and injury treatment.

Scope of practice

There is a lack of consistency in the definition and scope of practice of massage therapy among the regulated states. While most states have a well-defined scope of practice, there are still some states without massage therapy regulation. The National Certification Board for Therapeutic Massage & Bodywork (NCBTMB), the American Massage Therapy Association (AMTA), a 501(c)(6) professional association, and Associated Bodywork & Massage Professionals (ABMP), an influential membership organization in the field, all have interests related to various scopes of practice. While these interests overlap, they are not necessarily the same. One area where there is agreement is that massage specifically excludes diagnosis, prescription, manipulation or adjustments of the human skeletal structure, or any other service, procedure, or therapy requiring a different license to practice (e.g., orthopedics, physical therapy, podiatry, chiropractic, osteopathy, psychotherapy, acupuncture, or any other profession or branch of medicine).

Referral practices

Massage therapists are trained to know how and when to consult with medical doctors and other health professionals. Individual decisions must be made according to case circumstances and, in many instances, medical advice. Medications are a factor in considering how to design treatment plans. Clients may be allergic to certain oils/creams, or to cleansers/disinfectants used on sheets and tables. Presence of pins, staples, artificial joints, and pacemakers may alter treatment indications. Collaboration is necessary in emotional or psychiatric conditions, as massage is known to have an impact on these conditions.

Massage therapists do not diagnose. They are taught in school that there are conditions for which a full body massage treatment is contraindicated. The College of Massage Therapists of Ontario developed an extensive list of these conditions, which is available on its website at www.cmto.com.

Third-party payers

Third parties do reimburse for massage therapy; however, massage therapy is not covered in Centers for Medicare and Medicaid Services legislation. Payments are most often made for workers' compensation claims and auto accident injuries. Additional reimbursements vary by state and insurance provider. The state of Washington, for instance, mandates that all health plans include every category of licensed provider in their benefit design. Massage therapists are receiving an increasing number of referrals for healthcare treatments.

The AMTA holds a seat on the American Medical Association's CPT-HCPAC (Health Care Professionals Advisory Committee). This assures representation of the massage therapy profession in discussions of coding issues that may affect massage therapy. Issues involving insurance, such as the AMA CPT codes, are forwarded to the AMTA Board of Directors for consideration of what path would be in the best interest of the massage profession as a whole.

Integration Activities

A number of partnerships have developed between massage schools and medical schools. These partnerships can be as minimal as medical schools referring students to massage schools in the local area or as involved as jointly developing a curriculum for use in each other's institutions.

Education

Schools and programs

Of the 1,568 massage schools in the US, nearly 74% have programs of 500 hours or more. Of the total number of schools with a 500-hour program or more, 43% offer just 500 hours. In most cases, the total number of hours a school offers trends closely to what is required for state licensure, which varies from state to state.

The Council of Schools (COS) has been a member classification within the AMTA, with 385 member schools. Institutional AMTA memberships have been provided to schools. The status of this class of members is under discussion as of this writing. The Council of Schools is a network of massage school administrators, owners, and directors who provide counsel to the AMTA Board of Directors on issues directly related to schools. AMTA offers a teacher's track at the annual convention as well as a leadership conference for school administrators.

The ABMP has a Massage School Alliance with a staff of six professionals who work directly with the schools. They offer a school issues forum on an annual basis for schools to come together to discuss common challenges. There are no dues or fees associated with the Massage School Alliance.

Curriculum content

Unlike the other disciplines within ACCAHC, there are neither national standards nor a single recognized body that the whole profession has designated to determine the knowledge and skills required to call oneself a massage therapist. There exists, therefore, a wide variety in the type and quality of education available in massage schools and programs. At this time, there is no consensus regarding the required number of hours of study for entry-level massage, although 500 hours seems to be where the majority of schools land. Five hundred hours is the necessary minimum to sit for the national certification exam and is the required length for many state licenses.

Many practitioners choose to take continuing education courses to gain more extensive training in a specific modality or area. Requirements for continuing education vary from state to state depending on state licensure requirements, according to the membership organization a practitioner chooses to join, and depending on whether the practitioner elects to maintain the national certification credential.

Accreditation

There are three specialized accrediting agencies with curriculum standards for massage. The Commission on Massage Therapy Accreditation (COMTA) is the agency that was started by the massage profession and granted recognition by the US Department of Education in 2002; it is the primary specialized accreditor for massage therapy and bodywork. Several years later, the National Accrediting Commission of Cosmetology Arts and Sciences (NACCAS) was granted an expansion of scope to include massage therapy programs, primarily within cosmetology schools. The Accrediting Bureau of Health Education Schools (ABHES) also accredits massage programs, primarily within schools that offer other health-related vocational education programs.

Currently, there are 97 COMTA accredited schools and programs in the US and Canada. ABHES accredits approximately 50 schools and programs of massage therapy. The number of programs NACCAS accredits was not available at the time of publishing.

Regulation and Certification

Regulatory status

Forty-three states and the District of Columbia have some form of regulation in place for massage therapy; however, there is a lack of consistency among these licensure laws. Depending on the state law, massage therapists can be referred to as licensed, state certified, or registered. In most cases, only individuals who have the state designation may perform massage and/or use a title indicating that they perform massage.

Examinations and certifications

The National Certification Board for Therapeutic Massage & Bodywork (NCBTMB) is a nationally accredited credentialing body that administers a certification program that attests to the core knowledge and attributes expected of entry-level practitioners of therapeutic massage and bodywork. Founded in 1992, NCBTMB's mission is to define and advance the highest standards in the massage and bodywork profession. The certification program is more than just an exam, and requires adherence to the NCBTMB Code of

Ethics and Standards of Practice, continuing education, and recertification to ensure practitioners function in a manner that protects public health and safety.

NCBTMB offers two exams: the National Certification Examination for Therapeutic Massage and Bodywork (NCETMB) and a massage-specific exam, the National Certification Examination for Therapeutic Massage (NCETM). In keeping with best practices for certification, NCBTMB conducts job analyses every five years to ensure its test content remains relevant to current practice. NCBTMB conducted its fourth job analysis in 2007. The job task analysis is posted on the NCBTMB website at www.ncbtmb.org. There are over 90,000 nationally certified practitioners in the US.

Currently, NCBTMB examinations are used in 33 states and the District of Columbia in either statute or rule. In addition to its certifying exams, NCBTMB also offers a state licensing option called the National Examination for State Licensing (NESL). With the NESL, individual states are able to determine their own statutory (or adopted rule) educational requirements and/or criteria for practitioners, and still have a credible examination at their disposal.

The Federation of State Massage Therapy Boards (FSMTB), established in 2005, is currently made up of 32 state licensing boards and agencies that regulate the massage therapy and bodywork profession. The mission of the Federation is to support its member boards in their work to ensure that the practice of massage therapy is provided to the public in a safe and effective manner. In October 2007, FSMTB created an entry-level national licensure examination to serve the needs of the regulatory community in licensing massage therapists. A job task analysis (JTA) survey was developed and deployed online from October 13, 2006 until February 1, 2007. The FSMTB has published the detailed results on its website, www.fsmtb.org.

Currently, 19 states accept the FSMTB exam, 32 states accept the NCBTMB's examination program (some states accept both exams), and others have no testing requirements. For a state-by-state compendium of laws, please visit the AMTA website at www.amtamassage.org.

Research

The Massage Therapy Foundation's mission is to advance the knowledge and practice of massage therapy by supporting scientific research, education, and community service. The Foundation funds solid research studies investigating the many beneficial applications of massage therapy. Foundation research grants are awarded to individuals or teams conducting studies that promise to advance the understanding of specific therapeutic applications of massage, public perceptions of and attitudes toward massage therapy, and the role of massage therapy in healthcare delivery.

The Massage Therapy Foundation commissioned a research agenda in 1999, recommending areas of research in massage therapy and bodywork that are most needed. Investigators who apply for Foundation research grants are referred to the agenda and are encouraged to address one of the following areas in their research:

- Build a massage research infrastructure
- Fund studies into safety and efficacy
- Fund studies of physiological (or other) mechanisms (how massage works)
- Fund studies stemming from a wellness paradigm
- Fund studies into the profession of therapeutic massage and bodywork

The Massage Therapy Foundation launched the *International Journal of Therapeutic Massage and Bodywork: Research, Education and Practice* (IJTMB) in August, 2008. It is a free, online, peer-reviewed journal.

Another organization, the Massage Therapy Research Consortium, is a voluntary collaboration of massage schools that are interested in enhancing their own understanding of and participation in research on therapeutic massage. This group works to provide mutual support and to pool resources for joint educational and research activities. This group is working on a number of research projects involving the massage therapy profession.

In addition to its efficacy for muscle and other soft tissue ailments, research has shown that massage therapy can relieve symptoms associated with many serious health issues. Among the ways massage therapy has been shown to be effective are:

- **Relief of Back Pain**—More than 100 million Americans suffer from low-back pain, and nearly $25 billion a year is spent in search of relief. A 2003 study showed that massage therapy produced better results and reduced the need for painkillers by 36% when compared to other therapies, including acupuncture and spinal modification. Today, massage therapy is one of the most common ways people ease back pain.[1]

- **Treating Migraines**—Of the 45 million Americans who suffer from chronic headaches, more than 60% suffer from migraines. For many, it's a distressing disorder that is triggered by stress and poor sleep. In a recent study, massage therapy recipients exhibited fewer migraines and better sleep quality during the weeks they received massage, and the three weeks following, than did participants who did not receive massage therapy. Another study found that in adults with migraine headaches, massage therapy decreased the occurrence of headaches, sleep disturbances, and distress symptoms. It also increased serotonin levels, believed to play an important role in the regulation of mood, sleep, and appetite.[2, 3]

- **Easing Symptoms of Carpal Tunnel**—Carpal tunnel syndrome is a progressively painful condition that causes numbness and tingling in the thumb and middle fingers. Traditional treatments for carpal tunnel range from a wrist brace to surgery. However, a 2004 study found that carpal tunnel patients receiving massage reported significantly less pain, fewer symptoms, and improved grip strength compared to patients who did not receive massage.[4]

- **Reducing Depression and Anxiety**—An estimated 20 million Americans suffer from depression. A review of more than a dozen massage studies concluded that massage therapy helps relieve depression and anxiety by affecting the body's biochemistry. In the studies reviewed, researchers measured the stress hormone cortisol in participants before and immediately after massage and found that the therapy lowered levels by up to 53%. Massage also increased serotonin and dopamine, and neurotransmitters that help reduce depression.[5]

- **Alleviating Symptoms and Side Effects of Cancer**—Massage therapy is increasingly being applied to symptoms experienced by cancer patients, such as nausea, pain, and fatigue. Researchers at Memorial Sloan-Kettering Cancer Center asked patients to report the severity of their symptoms before and after receiving massage therapy. Patients reported reduced levels of anxiety, pain, fatigue, depression, and nausea, even up to two days later.[6] In a study of breast cancer patients, researchers found that those who were massaged three times a week reported lower levels of depression, anxiety and anger, while increasing natural killer cells and lymphocytes that help to battle cancerous tumors.[7, 8]

- **Lowering Blood Pressure**—Hypertension, if left unchecked, can lead to organ damage. Preliminary research shows that hypertensive patients who received three 10-minute back massages a week had a reduction in blood pressure, compared to patients who simply relaxed without a massage.[9]

Challenges and Opportunities

The following descriptions are intended to assist the reader in understanding aspects of the massage therapy profession; they do not represent specific positions on the issues.

Key challenges 2009–2012

- As mentioned earlier, there is currently inconsistent use of terminology and definitions within the massage therapy profession. To continue to move toward consistency within the profession, terminology will need to be standardized, which will ensure the accurate, professional description of massage therapy practice.
- Massage therapy educational programs also need to move to greater standardization in the content, scope, and length of entry-level training programs.
- Faculty qualifications vary greatly from school to school. There is currently no commonly agreed upon formal training for massage therapy instructors, but the need for training is also part of creating consistency in educational programs for massage therapy. Without consistency in educational programs and faculty qualifications, consistency in terminology will prove difficult and consumer expectations will also be affected.

Key opportunities 2009–2012

- Further development of industry partnerships with potential massage therapy employers will increase knowledge of massage therapy training and credentials among those industries, and provide more opportunities for collaboration in client care. Partnership with employers will, in turn, give the massage education institutions much needed information on what employers' needs are so curriculum can be developed to meet those needs and enhance the likelihood of job placement for graduates.

- Development of the profession's research base will allow practitioners to provide more effective, outcome-based massage therapy for their clients, which will provide better results and increase the demand for massage therapy. Establishing awareness of and interest in massage as an effective therapy will increase acceptance by healthcare providers and third-party payers. Greater communication within the profession will also increase as a standardized scientific language is more commonly used.

- As massage and bodywork become a more integral component of the complementary, alternative, and integrative aspects of health care, there will be an increasing demand for quality, standardization, and research. This demand will help set the parameters for the profession to evolve into a more recognized, valuable, and respected part of health care.

Resources

Organizations and websites
The profession is represented by a number of member organizations and one national certification organization:

- American Massage Therapy Association® (AMTA) represents more than 500 massage therapy schools and programs and has more than 58,000 member massage therapists. AMTA works to establish massage therapy as integral to the maintenance of good health and complementary to other therapeutic processes, and to advance the profession by promoting certification and school accreditation, ethics and standards, continuing education, professional publications, legislative efforts, public education, and fostering the development of members. AMTA offers liability insurance to its members.

- National Certification Board for Therapeutic Massage & Bodywork (NCBTMB) was founded in 1992 as a 501(c)(6) organization to establish a national certification program and uphold a national standard of professionalism. NCBTMB works to foster high standards of ethical and professional practice through a recognized, credible credentialing program that assures the competency of practitioners of therapeutic massage and bodywork. NCBTMB also has outreach programs for stakeholders, including schools and state boards. The organization had certified more than 90,000 massage therapists and bodyworkers as of the date of publication of this booklet. NCBTMB's certification program is made up of a number of components: eligibility, examinations, Code of Ethics, Standards of Practice, continuing education and recertification. NCBTMB's certification program is accredited by the National Commission for Certifying Agencies (NCCA), the accrediting branch of the National Organization for Competency Assurance (NOCA).

- Associated Bodywork & Massage Professionals (ABMP), founded in 1987, is a for-profit organization with 64,000 client members. It offers publications and websites, support aimed at practice development needs, sharing of information on massage with the public, and advocacy for massage therapy laws and regulation. ABMP's Massage School Alliance communicates with over 1,000 training institutions and has responded to recent school quality challenges by developing supports for teaching faculty and students. ABMP also played an instrumental role in helping to create the Federation of State Massage Therapy Boards (FSMTB). ABMP offers liability insurance to its members.

- The Federation of State Massage Therapy Boards (FSMTB) was formed in 2005 to bring the regulatory community together and provide a forum for the exchange of information. The result of the exchange was the development of a licensure exam which was introduced in 2007. The FSMTB's mission is to support its member boards in their work to ensure that the practice of massage therapy is provided to the public in a safe and effective manner. There are currently 28 member boards with 13 states accepting the exam for licensing.

- Accrediting Bureau of Health Education Schools (ABHES) www.abhes.org
- American Massage Therapy Association (AMTA) www.amtamassage.org
- Associated Bodywork & Massage Professionals (ABMP) www.abmp.com

- Commission on Massage Therapy Accreditation (COMTA)
  www.comta.org
- Federation of State Massage Therapy Boards (FSMTB)
  www.fsmtb.org
- Massage Therapy Foundation
  www.massagetherapyfoundation.org
- Massage Therapy Research Consortium
  www.massagetherapyresearchconsortium.com
- National Accrediting Commission of Cosmetology Arts &
  Sciences (NACCAS)
  www.naccas.org
- National Certification Board for Therapeutic Massage &
  Bodywork (NCBTMB)
  www.ncbtmb.org

Citations

1. Cherkin DC, Sherman KJ, Deyo RA, Shekelle PG. A review of the evidence for the effectiveness, safety, and cost of acupuncture, massage therapy, and spinal manipulation for back pain. *Ann Intern Med.* 2003;138(11): 898-906.
2. Lawler SP, Cameron LD. A randomized, controlled trial of massage therapy as a treatment for migraine. *Ann Behav Med.* 2006;32(1):50-9.
3. Hernandez-Reif M, Dieter J, Field F, et al. Migraine headaches are reduced by massage therapy. *Int J Neurosci.* 1998; 96(1):1-11.
4. Field T, Diego M, Cullen C, et al. Carpal tunnel syndrome symptoms are lessened following massage therapy. *J Bodywork and Movement Ther.* 2004;8(1):9-14.
5. Field T, Hernandez-Reif M, Miguel Diego M, et al. Cortisol decreases and serotonin and dopamine increase following massage therapy. *Int J Neurosci.* 2005;115(10):1397-1413.
6. Cassileth BR, Vickers AJ. Massage therapy for symptom control: outcome study at a major cancer center. *J Pain Symptom Manage.* 2004;28(3):244-9.
7. Hernandez-Reif M, Field F, Ironson G, et al. Natural killer cells and lymphocytes increase in women with breast cancer following massage therapy. *Int J Neurosci.* 2005;115(4): 495-510.
8. Hernandez-Reif M, Ironson G, Field T, et al. Breast cancer patients have improved immune and neuroendocrine functions following massage therapy. *J Psychosom Res.* 2004; 57(1):45-52.
9. Moyer CA, Rounds J, Hannum J. A meta analysis of massage therapy research. *Psychol Bull.* 2004:130(1):3-18.
10. Olney CM. The effect of therapeutic back massage in hypertensive persons: a preliminary study. *Biol Res Nurs.* 2005;7(2):98-105.

Bibliography

Benjamin BE, Sohnen-Moe C. *The Ethics of Touch*. Tucson, AZ: Sohnen-Moe Associates; 2003.

Benjamin P, Tappan F. *Tappan's Handbook of Healing Massage Techniques: Classic, Holistic, and Emerging Methods*. 5th ed. Boston, MA: Pearson Education; 2009.

Biel A, Dorn R. *Trail Guide to the Body*. 3rd ed. Boulder, CO: Books of Discovery; 2005.

Cohen B. *Memmler's The Human Body in Health and Disease*. 10th ed. Philadelphia, PA: Lippincott Williams & Wilkins; 2005.

Fritz S. *Fundamentals of Therapeutic Massage*. 4th ed. St. Louis, MO: Mosby; 2009.

Frye B. *Body Mechanics for Manual Therapists: A Functional Approach to Self-Care*. 2nd ed. Stanwood, Washington: Fryetag; 2004.

Hymel GM. *Research Methods for Massage and Holistic Therapies*. St. Louis, MO: Mosby; 2006.

Lowe W. *Orthopedic Massage: Theory and Technique*. St. Louis, MO: Elsevier Health Services; 2003.

Menard MB. *Making Sense of Research: A Guide to Research Literacy for Complementary Practitioners*. Toronto, Ontario, Canada: Curties-Overzet; 2003.

Rattray F, Ludwig L. *Clinical Massage Therapy: Understanding, Assessing and Treating Over 70 Conditions*. Elora, Ontario, Canada: Talus; 2000.

Sohnen-Moe C. *Business Mastery: A Guide for Creating a Fulfilling, Thriving Business and Keeping it Successful*. Tucson, AZ: Sohnen-Moe Associates; 2008.

Thompson DL. *Hands Heal: Communication, Documentation, and Insurance Billing for Manual Therapists*. 3rd ed. Philadelphia, PA: Lippincott, Williams & Wilkins; 2006.

Werner R. *A Massage Therapist's Guide to Pathology*. 4th ed. Philadelphia, PA: Lippincott, Williams & Wilkins; 2008.

Williams A, ed. *Teaching Massage: Fundamental Principles in Adult Education for Massage Program Instructors*. Philadelphia, PA: Lippincott, Williams & Wilkins; 2008.

Yates J. *A Physician's Guide to Therapeutic Massage*. Toronto, Ontario, Canada: Curties-Overzet; 2004.

Direct-entry Midwifery

Jo Anne Myers-Ciecko, MPH

Partner Organization: Midwifery Education Accreditation Council (MEAC)

About the Author: Myers-Ciecko is the executive director for MEAC.

Philosophy, Mission, and Goals

Midwives work in partnership with women to give the necessary support, care, and advice during pregnancy, labor and the postpartum period, to conduct births on the midwife's own responsibility, and to provide care for the newborn and the infant. This care includes preventive measures, the promotion of normal birth, the detection of complications in mother and child, the accessing of medical or other appropriate assistance, and the carrying out of emergency measures.

Midwives have an important task in health counseling and education, not only for the woman, but also within the family and community. This work involves prenatal education and preparation for parenthood, and may extend to women's health, sexual or reproductive health, and childcare. (Excerpts from the International Confederation of Midwives definition of a midwife)

Direct-entry midwifery refers to an educational path that does not require prior nursing training to enter the profession. Certified Professional Midwives (CPMs) are direct-entry midwives who are nationally certified, a credential first awarded in 1994. The National Association of Certified Professional Midwives (NACPM) was founded in 2000 to increase women's access to midwives by supporting the work and practice of CPMs. NACPM adopted the following *Philosophy and Principles of Practice* in 2004:

1. NACPM Members respect the mystery, sanctity, and potential for growth inherent in the experience of pregnancy and birth.

2. NACPM members understand birth to be a pivotal life event for mother, baby, and family. It is the goal of midwifery care to support and empower the mother and to protect the natural process of birth.

3. Members of NACPM respect the biological integrity of the processes of pregnancy and birth as aspects of a woman's sexuality.

4. Members of NACPM recognize the inseparable and interdependent relationship of the mother-baby pair.

5. NACPM members believe that responsible and ethical midwifery care respects the life of the baby by nurturing and respecting the mother, and, when necessary, counseling and educating her in ways to improve fetal/infant well-being.

6. NACPM members work as autonomous practitioners, recognizing that this autonomy makes possible a true partnership with the women they serve and enables them to bring a broad range of skills to the partnership.

7. NACPM members recognize that decision making involves a synthesis of knowledge, skills, intuition, and judgment.

8. Members of NACPM know that the best research demonstrates that out-of-hospital birth is a safe and rational choice for healthy women, and that the out-of-hospital setting provides optimal opportunity for the empowerment of the mother and the support and protection of the normal process of birth.

9. NACPM members recognize that the mother or baby may on occasion require medical consultation or collaboration.

10. NACPM members recognize that optimal care of women and babies during pregnancy and birth takes place within a network of relationships with other care providers who can provide service outside the scope of midwifery practice when needed.

While NACPM represents CPMs, the Midwives Alliance of North America (MANA), founded in 1982, is a broad-based alliance representing the breadth and diversity of the profession of midwifery in the United States. Members include Certified Professional Midwives as well as Certified Nurse-Midwives (CNMs), state-licensed midwives, and traditional midwives who serve special populations such as the Amish or indigenous communities. MANA adopted "Core Competencies for Basic Midwifery Practice," in 1994, including the following *Guiding Principles*:

1. Midwives work in partnership with women and their chosen support community throughout the caregiving relationship.
2. Midwives respect the dignity, rights, and the ability of the women they serve to act responsibly throughout the caregiving relationship.
3. Midwives work as autonomous practitioners, collaborating with other health and social service providers when necessary.
4. Midwives understand that physical, emotional, psychosocial and spiritual factors synergistically comprise the health of individuals and affect the childbearing process.
5. Midwives understand that female physiology and childbearing are normal processes, and work to optimize the well-being of mothers and their developing babies as the foundation of caregiving.
6. Midwives understand that the childbearing experience is primarily a personal, social, and community event.
7. Midwives recognize that a woman is the only direct care provider for herself and her unborn baby; thus, the most important determinant of a healthy pregnancy is the mother herself.
8. Midwives recognize the empowerment inherent in the childbearing experience and strive to support women to make informed decisions and take responsibility for their own well-being.
9. Midwives strive to insure vaginal birth and provide guidance and support when appropriate to facilitate the spontaneous process of pregnancy, labor, and birth, utilizing medical intervention only as necessary.
10. Midwives synthesize clinical observations, theoretical knowledge, intuitive assessment, and spiritual awareness as components of a competent decision-making process.
11. Midwives value continuity of care throughout the childbearing cycle and strive to maintain continuous care within realistic limits.

12. Midwives understand that the parameters of "normal" vary widely and recognize that each pregnancy and birth is unique.

Characteristics and Data

There are more than 1,500 Certified Professional Midwives. Information on the number of direct-entry midwives who are not CPMs is not available, though estimates range from 500 to 3,000. CPMs are typically self-employed, working in small, community-based practices. There are approximately 8,000 Certified Nurse-Midwives practicing in the US. Most CNMs practice in hospitals, while virtually all CPMs attend births in the client's home or free-standing birth centers. Direct-entry midwives own half of all birth centers in the country.

Clinical Care

Approach to patient care

Midwifery care encompasses the normal childbearing cycle of pregnancy, birth, and postpartum care. NACPM, MANA, and other leading organizations that support direct-entry midwifery endorse the following statement:

The *Midwives Model of Care*™ is based on the fact that pregnancy and birth are normal life events. The Midwives Model of Care includes:

- monitoring the physical, psychological and social well-being of the mother throughout the childbearing cycle
- providing the mother with individualized education, counseling, and prenatal care, continuous hands-on assistance during labor and delivery, and postpartum support
- minimizing technological interventions
- identifying and referring women who require obstetrical attention

The application of this model has been proven to reduce to incidence of birth injury, trauma, and cesarean section (Hatem, et al. 2007, Sakala and Cory 2008, Kennedy 2000, Rooks 1999, Janssen 2002, Johnson and Daviss 2005, Health Management Associates 2007).

Researchers who interviewed direct-entry midwives early in the development of the home-birth movement found that a wellness orientation, shared responsibility, passive management, holistic care, and individualized care were central to the midwifery approach to care (Sullivan and Weitz, 1988). Exemplary midwifery practice was described by clients, direct-entry midwives, and nurse-midwives in another study that identified critical process-of-care qualities such as supporting the normalcy of birth, respecting the uniqueness of the woman and family, vigilance and attention to detail, and creating a setting that is respectful and reflects the woman's needs (Kennedy, 2000).

Scope of practice

The National Association of Certified Professional Midwives (NACPM) defines the midwives' scope of practice as providing expert care, education, counseling, and support to women and their families throughout the caregiving partnership, including pregnancy, birth, and postpartum. NACPM members provide ongoing care throughout pregnancy and continuous, hands-on care during labor, birth, and the immediate postpartum period. They are trained to recognize abnormal or dangerous conditions needing expert help outside their scope and to consult or refer as necessary.

The North American Registry of Midwives (NARM) recognizes that each midwife is an individual with specific practice protocols that reflect her own style and philosophy, level of experience, and legal status, and that practice guidelines may vary with each midwife. NARM does not set protocols for all CPMs to follow, but requires that they develop their own practice guidelines in written form.

In certain jurisdictions, the midwives' scope of practice includes well-woman care and family planning services. Midwives may also administer certain drugs and devices as specified in state law, including IV fluids, antibiotics, local anesthetic, antihemorrhagics for postpartum use, etc. Midwives typically carry oxygen and resuscitation equipment and are certified in adult and neonatal resuscitation.

Referral practices

Direct-entry midwives care for essentially healthy women expecting normal pregnancy, birth, and postpartum experiences. Midwives consult with and refer to an array of healthcare professionals, social service providers, and others whose services may benefit the woman and her family. These include, but are not limited to, allopathic physicians, naturopathic physicians, acupuncturists, chiropractors, massage therapists, childbirth educators, psychologists, family therapists, doulas, nutritionists, social workers, and food support and housing agencies. In some states, midwives are legally obligated to consult with and/or refer women to obstetricians or family physicians with obstetrical privileges when certain conditions arise. In addition, because the vast majority of direct-entry midwives attend births in their clients' homes or in freestanding birth centers, any complications that require hospitalization for labor and/or birth necessitate transfer of care to an obstetrical care provider with hospital privileges. Most transfers are non-emergent, resulting from a failure to progress in labor, the mother's desire for pain relief, or maternal exhaustion. Less common but more urgent indications include preeclampsia, maternal hemorrhage, retained placenta, malpresentation, sustained fetal distress, and respiratory problems in the newborn.

Third-party payers

Direct-entry midwives are reimbursed by private insurance plans and contract with managed care organizations in many states. A few states mandate reimbursement under "every category of provider" or "any willing provider" laws. At least ten states reimburse direct-entry midwives for services provided to women on Medicaid. This is a high-priority issue for the National Association of Certified Professional Midwives, which is committed to achieving national recognition for the CPM, including mandatory inclusion in Medicaid programs.

Integration Activities

The National Association of Certified Professional Midwives is represented in numerous national organizations and initiatives focused on healthcare reform and women's health issues. These include the Integrated Healthcare Policy Consortium, Health Care for America Now, and the National Quality Forum.

MANA is a member of the Coalition for Improving Maternity Services, a broad-based coalition of over 50 organizations, representing over 90,000 members. The coalition's mission is to promote a wellness model of maternity care that will improve birth outcomes and substantially reduce costs. MANA is also a partner in The Safe Motherhood Initiatives-USA, a partnership of organizations whose goal is to reduce maternal mortality in the United States.

In 2008, the Indian Health Service, in the US Department of Health and Human Services, co-sponsored an "Invitational Gathering on North American Indigenous Birthing and Midwifery," which brought together key participants in indigenous birthing and midwifery from Canada and the US to share information and promising practices, and to identify potential areas of collaboration and partnerships. Representatives of MANA, NARM, and the Midwifery Education Accreditation Council (MEAC) attended to report on the CPM credential, educational pathways, and accreditation.

In 2006, the White Ribbon Alliance for Safe Motherhood convened a national working group to develop guidelines to ensure that the healthcare needs of pregnant women, new mothers, fragile newborns, and infants would be adequately met during and after a disaster. They recommended that CPMs should be engaged in local and regional planning efforts, that home-birth skills should be taught to all providers, and that information be provided on how to prepare for birth outside the hospital.

In 2001 the American Public Health Association adopted a resolution supporting "Increasing Access To Out-Of-Hospital Maternity Care Services Through State-Regulated and Nationally-Certified Direct-Entry Midwives." APHA supports licensing and certification for direct-entry midwives, increased funding for scholarship and loan repayment programs, and eliminating barriers to the reimbursement and equitable payment of direct-entry midwives. (For complete document see http://www.cfmidwifery.org/pdf/apha.pdf.)

In 1999 the Pew Health Professions Commission and the UCSF Center for the Health Professions issued a joint report on "The Future of Midwifery" calling for expanding educational opportunities for both nurse-midwifery and direct-entry midwifery, health policies that facilitate integration of midwifery services, and research to evaluate practices. (For complete document see http://www.futurehealth.ucsf.edu/Content/29/1999-04_Charting_a_Course_%20for_the_21st_Century_The_Future_of_Midwifery.pdf.)

There are now two midwifery education programs located in state-funded colleges and another in development. Faculty from other direct-entry programs are often invited to lecture in medical and nursing programs.

Education

Schools and Programs

There are currently eleven MEAC-accredited schools and programs, including three degree-granting institutions, two programs located within universities, and seven schools offering certificate programs. Several offer distance learning courses in combination with clinical preceptorships. Three of the free-standing schools and both of the university-based programs participate in US Department of Education Title IV financial aid programs. There are nearly 600 students enrolled in accredited midwifery programs and institutions. In addition, there are probably that many more independent students who are completing community-based apprenticeships, following guidelines provided by NARM, whose training will be assessed individually through NARM's Portfolio Evaluation Process.

Accredited programs (July 2009):
- Bastyr University, Department of Naturopathic Midwifery, Kenmore, WA
  http://www.bastyr.edu/academic/naturopath/midwifery/
- Miami Dade College, Midwifery Sciences Department, Miami, FL
  http://www.mdc.edu/medical/Nursing/Programs/Midwifery_Prog/main.htm

Accredited institutions (July 2009):
- Birthingway College of Midwifery, Portland, OR
  http://www.birthingway.edu/
- Birthwise Midwifery School, Bridgton, ME
  http://www.birthwisemidwifery.org/
- Florida School of Traditional Midwifery, Gainesville, FL
  http://www.midwiferyschool.org
- Maternidad La Luz, El Paso, TX
  http://www.maternidadlaluz.com/
- Midwives College of Utah, Salt Lake City, UT
  http://www.midwifery.edu/
- National College of Midwifery, Taos, NM
  http://www.midwiferycollege.org/
- National Midwifery Institute, Bristol, VT
  http://www.nationalmidwiferyinstitute.com/

- Nizhoni Institute of Midwifery, Bonita, CA
  http://www.midwiferyatnizhoni.com/
- Seattle Midwifery School, Seattle, WA
  http://www.seattlemidwifery.org/

Curriculum content
The *MANA Core Competencies for Basic Midwifery Practice* address the following content (in addition to the guiding principles mentioned elsewhere in this chapter):

General knowledge and skills
The midwife provides care incorporating certain concepts, skills, and knowledge from a variety of health and social sciences, including, but not limited to:

1. Communication, counseling, and teaching skills
2. Human anatomy and physiology relevant to childbearing
3. Community standards of care for women and their developing infants during the childbearing cycle, including midwifery and bio-technical medical standards and the rationale for and limitations of such standards
4. Health and social resources in her community
5. Significance of and methods for documentation of care through the childbearing cycle
6. Informed decision making
7. The principles and appropriate application of clean and aseptic technique and universal precautions
8. Human sexuality, including indications of common problems and indications for counseling
9. Ethical considerations relevant to reproductive health
10. The grieving process
11. Knowledge of cultural variations
12. Knowledge of common medical terms
13. The ability to develop, implement, and evaluate an individualized plan for midwifery care
14. Woman-centered care, including the relationship between the mother, infant, and their larger support community
15. Knowledge and application of various healthcare modalities as they apply to the childbearing cycle

Care during pregnancy

The midwife provides health care, support, and information to women throughout pregnancy. She determines the need for consultation or referral as appropriate. The midwife uses a foundation of knowledge and/or skill which includes the following:

1. Identification, evaluation, and support of maternal and fetal well-being throughout the process of pregnancy
2. Education and counseling for the childbearing cycle
3. Preexisting conditions in a woman's health history which are likely to influence her well-being when she becomes pregnant
4. Nutritional requirements of pregnant women and methods of nutritional assessment and counseling
5. Changes in emotional, psychosocial, and sexual variations that may occur during pregnancy
6. Environmental and occupational hazards for pregnant women
7. Methods of diagnosing pregnancy
8. Basic understanding of genetic factors which may indicate the need for counseling, testing, or referral
9. Basic understanding of the growth and development of the unborn baby
10. Indications for, risks, and benefits of bio-technical screening methods and diagnostic tests used during pregnancy
11. Anatomy, physiology, and evaluation of the soft and bony structures of the pelvis
12. Palpation skills for evaluation of the fetus and uterus
13. The causes, assessment, and treatment of the common discomforts of pregnancy
14. Identification of, implications of, and appropriate treatment for various infections, disease conditions, and other problems which may affect pregnancy
15. Special needs of the Rh- woman

Care during labor, birth, and immediately thereafter

The midwife provides health care, support, and information to women throughout labor, birth, and the hours immediately thereafter. She determines the need for consultation or referral as appropriate. The midwife uses a foundation of knowledge and/or skill which includes the following:

1. The normal process of labor and birth
2. Parameters and methods for evaluating maternal and fetal well-being during labor, birth, and immediately thereafter, including relevant historical data
3. Assessment of the birthing environment, assuring that it is clean, safe and supportive, and that appropriate equipment and supplies are on hand
4. Emotional responses and their impact during labor, birth, and immediately thereafter
5. Comfort and support measures during labor, birth, and immediately thereafter
6. Fetal and maternal anatomy and their interactions as relevant to assessing fetal position and the progress of labor
7. Techniques to assist and support the spontaneous vaginal birth of the baby and placenta
8. Fluid and nutritional requirements during labor, birth, and immediately thereafter
9. Assessment of and support for maternal rest and sleep as appropriate during the process of labor, birth, and immediately thereafter
10. Causes of, evaluation of, and appropriate treatment for variations which occur during the course of labor, birth, and immediately thereafter
11. Emergency measures and transport for critical problems arising during labor, birth, or immediately thereafter
12. Understanding of and appropriate support for the newborn's transition during the first minutes and hours following birth
13. Familiarity with current bio-technical interventions and technologies which may be commonly used in a medical setting
14. Evaluation and care of the perineum and surrounding tissues

Postpartum care

The midwife provides health care, support, and information to women throughout the postpartum period. She determines the need for consultation or referral as appropriate. The midwife uses a foundation of knowledge and/or skill which includes but is not limited to the following:

1. Anatomy and physiology of the mother during the postpartum period
2. Lactation support and appropriate breast care including evaluation of, identification of, and treatments for problems with nursing
3. Parameters and methods for evaluating and promoting maternal well-being during the postpartum period
4. Causes of, evaluation of, and treatment for maternal discomforts during the postpartum period
5. Emotional, psychosocial, and sexual variations during the postpartum period
6. Maternal nutritional requirements during the postpartum period including methods of nutritional evaluation and counseling
7. Causes of, evaluation of, and treatments for problems arising during the postpartum period
8. Support, information, and referral for family planning methods as the individual woman desires

Newborn care

The entry-level midwife provides health care to the newborn during the postpartum period and support and information to parents regarding newborn care. She determines the need for consultation or referral as appropriate. The midwife uses a foundation of knowledge and/or skill which includes the following:

1. Anatomy, physiology, and support of the newborn's adjustment during the first days and weeks of life
2. Parameters and methods for evaluating newborn wellness including relevant historical data and gestational age
3. Nutritional needs of the newborn
4. Community standards and state laws regarding indications for, administration of, and the risks and benefits of prophylactic bio-technical treatments and screening tests commonly used during the neonatal period
5. Causes of, assessment of, appropriate treatment, and emergency measures for neonatal problems and abnormalities

Professional, legal, and other aspects

The entry-level midwife assumes responsibility for practicing in accord with the principles outlined in this document. The midwife uses a foundation of knowledge and/or skill which includes the following:

1. MANA's documents concerning the art and practice of midwifery
2. The purpose and goal of MANA and local (state or provincial) midwifery associations
3. The principles of data collection as relevant to midwifery practice
4. Laws governing the practice of midwifery in her local jurisdiction
5. Various sites, styles, and modes of practice within the larger midwifery community
6. A basic understanding of maternal/child healthcare delivery systems in her local jurisdiction
7. Awareness of the need for midwives to share their knowledge and experience

Woman care and family planning

Depending upon education and training, the entry-level midwife may provide family planning and well-woman care. The practicing midwife may also choose to meet the following core competencies with additional training. In either case, the midwife provides care, support, and information to women regarding their overall reproductive health, using a foundation of knowledge and/or skill which includes the following:

1. Understanding of the normal life cycle of women
2. Evaluation of the woman's well-being including relevant historical data
3. Causes of, evaluation of, and treatments for problems associated with the female reproductive system and breasts
4. Information on, provision of, or referral for various methods on contraception
5. Issues involved in decision making regarding unwanted pregnancies and resources for counseling and referral

Accreditation

The Midwifery Education Accreditation Council (MEAC) is recognized by the US Secretary of Education as the accrediting agency for direct-entry midwifery education programs. All

MEAC-accredited institutions and programs offer comprehensive programs that prepare graduates to become Certified Professional Midwives (CPMs). Most of the accredited programs are three years in length.

The standards for accreditation address curriculum requirements, faculty qualifications, facilities and students services, fiscal responsibility and administrative capacity. MEAC accreditation requires that the curriculum incorporate the MANA Core Competencies as well as the essential knowledge and skills identified by NARM. The clinical component must be at least one year in duration and must include specific clinical experience requirements. Programs must provide evidence that graduates are capable of passing the NARM written examination and becoming CPMs and/ or meeting the requirements for state licensure.

Regulation and Certification

Regulatory status

Direct-entry midwives are licensed or otherwise legally recognized practitioners in Alaska, Arkansas, Arizona, California, Colorado, Delaware, Florida, Idaho, Louisiana, Maine, Minnesota, Montana, New Hampshire, New Jersey, New Mexico, New York, Oregon, Rhode Island, South Carolina, Tennessee, Texas, Utah, Vermont, Virginia, Washington, and Wisconsin. All of these states (except New York) use the NARM written examination in their state regulatory process and/or recognize the CPM credential. A few states also require that applicants complete an accredited education program. Direct-entry midwives practice independently in most of these jurisdictions. Some state laws stipulate conditions requiring consultation or referral and others do not. Many provide a formulary of prescriptive drugs and devices that midwives may obtain and administer. Current information, including access to individual state laws, is available at http://www.mana.org/statechart.html.

Examinations and certifications

Certified Professional Midwives must demonstrate that they have met the minimum education, skills, and experience requirements set forth by the North American Registry of Midwives. Students must participate in a minimum of 40 births, including 20 births where the student functions in the role of primary midwife

under supervision, 10 births in homes or other out-of-hospital settings, and at least 3 births where the student also provided primary
care during the prenatal and postpartum periods. To establish their
qualifications, students must complete an accredited educational
program or undertake a portfolio evaluation process administered
by NARM to verify that their educational preparation included the
requisite knowledge, skills, and experiences.

The North American Registry of Midwives (NARM) is the certifying agency for CPMs. Certification is a credential that validates
the knowledge, skills, and abilities vital to responsible midwifery
practice, and that reflects and preserves the essential nature of
midwifery care. The CPM credential is unique among maternity
care providers in the US as it requires training and experience in
out-of-hospital birth. The NARM certification process recognizes
multiple routes of entry into midwifery and includes verification of
knowledge and skills and the successful completion of both a written examination and skills assessment. NARM conducts periodic
surveys of CPMs and completes a national job analysis to assure
that the examination is based on real-life job requirements. Candidates for certification must be graduates of an accredited program
or must complete a Portfolio Evaluation Process administered by
NARM. Certification is renewed every three years and all CPMs
must obtain continuing education and participate in peer review
for recertification.

The CPM credential is accredited by the National Commission
for Certifying Agencies (NCCA) which is the accrediting body of
the National Organization for Competency Assurance (NOCA).
NCCA encourages their accredited certification programs to have
an education evaluation process so candidates who have been educated outside of established pathways may have their qualifications evaluated for credentialing. The NARM Portfolio Evaluation
Process meets this recommendation.

Research

There is a growing body of evidence that points to the many
benefits of midwifery care. In October 2008, the Milbank Memorial
Fund released *Evidence-Based Maternity Care: What It Is and What It
Can Achieve*. The report presented best evidence that, if widely implemented, would have a positive impact on many mothers and babies and would improve value for payers. The report also identified

barriers to providing evidence-based maternity care, and made policy recommendations to address the barriers. Care provided by Certified Professional Midwives, documented in a landmark study of CPMs published in 2005, was highlighted in the Milbank Report: "The low CPM rates of intervention are benchmarks for what the majority of childbearing women and babies who are in good health might achieve."

An international review of the literature published by The Cochrane Collaboration in October 2008 found that "Midwife-led care was associated with several benefits for mothers and babies, and had no identified adverse effects. The main benefits were a reduced risk of losing a baby before 24 weeks. Also during labor, there was a reduced use of regional analgesia, with fewer episiotomies or instrumental births. Midwife-led care also increased the woman's chance of being cared for in labor by a midwife she had got to know. It also increased the chance of a spontaneous vaginal birth and initiation of breastfeeding. In addition, midwife-led care led to more women feeling they were in control during labor. There was no difference in risk of a mother losing her baby after 24 weeks." The review concluded that all women should be offered midwife-led models of care.

Another comprehensive review of the scientific evidence underlying the Coalition for Improving Maternity Services (CIMS), "Ten Steps of Mother-Friendly Care," was published in 2007. The authors found that equally good or better outcomes can be achieved in low-risk women having planned home births or giving birth in freestanding birth centers.

An economic cost-benefit analysis of direct-entry midwifery licensing and practice was undertaken in 2007 at the request of the Washington State Department of Health. The researchers determined that planned out-of-hospital births attended by professional midwives had similar rates of intrapartum and neonatal mortality to those of low-risk hospital births. They also found that medical intervention rates for planned out-of-hospital births were lower than planned low-risk hospital births. Using conservative cost estimates, they estimated the cost savings to the healthcare system (public and private insurance) was $2.7 million per biennium and recovery from Medicaid fee-for-service alone was more than $473,000 per biennium. These cost savings were achieved by licensed midwives attending just 2% of all births in the state.

Midwives Alliance of North America data collection has been ongoing since 1993 and includes a complete set of prospective data contributed by CPMs during the year 2000, when NARM required their participation. MANA established a Division of Research in 2004; it is charged with administering an online data-entry system, establishing research priorities, promoting publication, and providing education on research concepts and methods. A new web-based data collection system was launched in November 2004 and allows midwives to enter and review their own practice data as well as compiling data from all practices. Researchers will be able to use this unique system to study various aspects of midwifery care. Experts from the Centers for Disease Control have shown an interest in this database as it may now be the only repository of normal birth data in the country.

Challenges and Opportunities

Key challenges 2009–2012
- Securing legislation in states where midwifery is not recognized or is currently illegal
- Expanding job opportunities and third party reimbursement for direct-entry midwives
- Increasing the number of direct-entry midwifery education programs and opportunities for training
- Capacity building and fund development to support new and ongoing professional organization activities
- Coordinated and effective response to the increasing medicalization of pregnancy and birth, including the rapidly rising cesarean-section rate
- Preserving and promoting the principles, values, and practices of midwifery within the context of continuing professionalization of the home-birth and midwifery movements

Key opportunities 2009–2012
- NACPM, MANA, and related organizations are engaged in state and national health reform initiatives.
- MANA has launched a national public education campaign to raise public awareness and demand for midwifery services.
- MANA Division of Research continues ongoing and new research projects that compile information about and evaluate

midwifery practices, expand the knowledge base, and inform women's choices in maternity care and health policy decisions.

- As the majority of states now recognize direct-entry midwifery, there are more and more opportunities to promote this profession as a high-quality, cost-effective option in any health system (public or private payers, community health centers, etc.).

Resources

Organizations and websites

The National Association of Certified Professional Midwives (NACPM) was incorporated in 2000 to "empower and care for women as they make choices about their pregnancies and births, through the development and growth of the profession of midwifery." The NACPM strives to ensure that midwifery as practiced by CPMs will take its rightful place in the delivery of maternity care to women and families in the United States. Participation in healthcare reform and federal recognition of the CPM are current priorities for the NACPM.

The Midwives Alliance of North America (MANA) was founded in 1982 to form an identifiable and cohesive organization representing the profession of midwifery. MANA supported the creation of national standards for the certification of midwives. The certification process is administered by the North American Registry of Midwives and results in the credential Certified Professional Midwife (CPM). However, MANA does not require that members be certified and has an ongoing commitment to be an inclusive organization accessible to all midwives, regardless of their credential or legal status. MANA oversees numerous projects, including legislative advocacy, international relations, and public relations. The MANA Division of Research maintains a web-based system for prospective data collection that is a resource to midwives and other researchers interested in the processes and outcomes of midwifery care.

The Association of Midwifery Educators was launched in 2006 to strengthen schools and support midwifery educators. They publish a newsletter which has addressed topics ranging from faculty qualifications to student admissions practices. They also host a website and provide numerous opportunities for networking.

- American Association of Birth Centers
  www.birthcenters.org/
- American College of Nurse-Midwives
  www.acnm.org/
- Association of Midwifery Educators
  www.associationofmidwiferyeducators.org/
- Childbirth Connection
  www.childbirthconnection.org/
- Citizens for Midwifery
  www.cfmidwifery.org/
- Coalition for Improving Maternity Services
  www.motherfriendly.org/
- Foundation for the Advancement of Midwifery
  www.foundationformidwifery.org/
- International Confederation of Midwives
  www.internationalmidwives.org/
- Midwifery Education Accreditation Council
  www.meacschools.org/
- Midwives Alliance of North America
  www.mana.org/
- National Association of Certified Professional Midwives
  www.nacpm.org/
- North American Registry of Midwives
  www.narm.org/

Citations
Midwifery Model of Care
Kennedy H. A model of exemplary midwifery practice: results of a Delphi study. *J Midwifery Womens Health*. 2000;45(4):4-19.
Rooks, JP. The midwifery model of care. *J Nurse Midwifery*. 1999;44(4):370-374.

Midwifery education, professional associations, state regulation
Bourgeault I, Fynes M. Integrating lay and nurse-midwifery into the US and Canadian healthcare systems. *Soc Sci Med*. 1997;44(7):1051-1063.
Suarez SH. Midwifery is not the practice of medicine. *Yale J Law Fem*. 1993;5(2): 315-364.

Scope of practice, standards of practice, and quality assurance
Spindel PG, Suarez SH. Informed consent and home birth. *J Nurse Midwifery*. 1995;40(6):541-552.
Suarez SH. Midwifery is not the practice of medicine. *Yale J Law Fem*. 1993;5(2): 315-364.

Safety and cost-effectiveness of planned home birth

Health Management Associates. Midwifery Licensure and Discipline Program in Washington State: Economic Costs and Benefits. Midwives' Association of Washington State Web site. http://www.washingtonmidwives.org/assets/Midwifery_Cost_Study_10-31-07.pdf. 2007. Accessed November 17, 2009.

Janssen P, Lee SK, Ryan EM, et al. Outcomes of planned home births versus planned hospital births after regulation of midwifery in British Columbia. *CMAJ*. 2002;166(3):315-23.

Johnson KC, Daviss BA. Outcomes of planned home births with certified professional midwives: large prospective study in North America. *BMJ*. 2005; 330(7505):1416.

Consultation and referral

Davis-Floyd R. Home-birth emergencies in the US and Mexico: the trouble with transport. *Soc Sci Med*. 2003;56:1911-1931.

Stapleton SR. Team-building: making collaborative practice work. *J Nurse Midwifery*. 1998;43(1):12-18.

Bibliography
Selected books about midwifery and maternity care

Bridgman Perkins, B. *The Medical Delivery Business: Health Reform, Childbirth and the Economic Order*. Piscataway, NJ: Rutgers University Press; 2004.

Davis-Floyd R, Johnson CB, eds. *Mainstreaming Midwives: The Politics of Change*. New York, NY: Routledge; 2006.

Gaskin IM. *Ina May's Guide to Natural Childbirth*. New York, NY: Bantam; 2003.

Rooks JP. *Midwifery and Childbirth in America*. Philadelphia, PA: Temple University Press; 1999.

Rothman BK. *Laboring On: Birth in Transition in the United States*. New York, NY: Routledge; 2007.

Wagner M. *Born in the USA: How a Broken Maternity System Must Be Fixed to Put Women and Children First*. Berkeley, CA: University of California Press; 2006.

Reference texts

Cunningham FG, Gant NF, Leveno KJ, Gilstrap LC, Hauth JC, Wenstrom, KD. *William's Obstetrics*. 21st ed. New York, NY: McGraw-Hill; 2001.

Davis E. *Heart and Hands: A Midwife's Guide to Pregnancy and Birth*. 4th ed. Berkeley, CA: Celestial Arts; 2004.

Enkin M, Keirse M, Neilson J, et al. *A Guide to Effective Care in Pregnancy and Birth*. New York, NY: Oxford University Press; 2000.

Frye A. *Holistic Midwifery: A Comprehensive Textbook for Midwives and Home Birth Practice. Volume 1 – Care During Pregnancy*. Portland, OR: Labrys Press; 1995.

Frye A. *Holistic Midwifery: A Comprehensive Textbook for Midwives and Home Birth Practice. Volume 2 – Care During Labor and Birth*. Portland, OR: Labrys Press; 2004.

Frye A. *Understanding Diagnostic Tests in the Childbearing Year*. Portland, OR: Labrys Press; 1997.

Gaskin IM. *Spiritual Midwifery*. 4th ed. Summertown, TN: The Book Publishing Company; 2002.

Myles M. *Textbook for Midwives*. 14th ed. Philadelphia, PA: Elsevier; 2000.

Oxhorn H. *Human Labor and Birth.* 5th ed. New York, NY: McGraw-Hill; 1986.

Page LA. *The New Midwifery.* Philadelphia, PA: Churchill Livingstone; 2000.

Renfrew M, Fisher C, Arms S. *Bestfeeding: Getting Breastfeeding Right.* 2nd ed. Berkeley, CA: Celestial Arts; 2000.

Simkin P. *Labor Progress Handbook.* Cambridge, MA: Blackwell Scientific; 2000.

Sinclair C. *A Midwife's Handbook.* St. Louis, MO: Saunders; 2004.

Thureen P. *Assessment and Care of the Well Newborn.* St. Louis, MO: Saunders; 1998.

Varney H, Kriebs JM, Gegor CL. *Varney's Midwifery.* 4th ed. Sudbury, MA: Jones and Bartlett; 2004.

Weaver P, Evans S. *Practical Skills Guide for Midwifery.* 3rd ed. Wasilla, AK: Morningstar Publishing; 2001.

Wickham S. *Midwifery Best Practice.* Philadelphia, PA: Elsevier; 2003.

Reports and recommendations

Dower CM, Miller JE, O'Neil EH and the Taskforce on Midwifery. Charting a Course for the 21st Century: The Future of Midwifery. Center for the Health Professions at University of California San Francisco Web site. http://futurehealth.ucsf.edu/Content/29/1999-04_Charting_a_Course_%20for_the_21st_Century_The_Future_of_Midwifery.pdf. 1999. Accessed November 17, 2009.

Hatem M, Sandall J, Devane D, Soltani H, Gates S. Midwife-led versus other models of care for childbearing women. *Cochrane Database Syst Rev.* 2008;(4).

Lamaze International. The Coalition for Improving Maternity Services: Evidence Basis for the Ten Steps of Mother-Friendly Care. *Supp J Perinat Educ.* 2007;16(1).

Sakala C, Corry M. Evidence-Based Maternity Care: What It Is and What It Can Achieve. New York, NY: Milbank Memorial Fund; 2008.

The Mother-Friendly Childbirth Initiative. Coalition for Improving Maternity Services Web site. http://www.motherfriendly.org/mfci.php. 1996. Accessed November 17, 2009.

Wells S, Nelson C, Kotch JB, Weiss SH, Gaudino J. Increasing Access to Out-of-Hospital Maternity Care Services through State-Regulated, Nationally-Certified Direct-Entry Midwives. Midwives Alliance of North America Web site. http://mana.org/APHAformatted.pdf. 2001. Accessed November 17, 2009.

Naturopathic Medicine

Paul Mittman, ND, EdD, Patricia Wolfe, ND, Michael Traub, ND, DHANP

Partner Organization: Association of Accredited Naturopathic Medical Colleges (AANMC)

About the Authors: Mittman is president of Southwest College of Naturopathic Medicine and past president of the AANMC. Wolfe is director emeritus of the Boucher Institute of Naturopathic Medicine and a past AANMC member. Traub is a private practitioner and a past president of the American Association of Naturopathic Physicians.

Philosophy, Mission, and Goals

First conceived in 1902, naturopathic medicine is a holistic, coordinated approach to health care that respects the unique individuality of each person and that integrates modern biomedical sciences with a wide array of natural and conventional therapies. It is a comprehensive system of health care that integrates an array of modalities including clinical nutrition, botanical medicine, behavioral medicine, homeopathy, physical medicine (consisting of hydrotherapy and the application of heat, cold, light, electricity, ultrasound, and various hands-on techniques such as manipulation to correct stress or trauma in muscles, connective tissue, and the skeletal system), as well as clinical practices such as minor surgery, pharmacology, and obstetrics.[1] In addition, naturopathic physicians respect and apply the principles of a variety of traditional world medicines such as Ayurvedic medicine, aboriginal medicines, and Oriental medicine which, guided by meridian theory, incorporates Chinese herbology, needle and non-needle stimulation, and practices such as tai chi and qi gong to balance the flow of "chi " or "qi" through the meridians. Naturopathic physicians encourage the inherent self-healing abilities of the individual through lifestyle education and the application of non-suppressive therapeutic methods and modalities.

The American Association of Naturopathic Physicians (AANP) defines naturopathic medicine as: "a distinct system of primary health care—an art, science, philosophy and practice of diagnosis, treatment, and prevention of illness. Naturopathic medicine is distinguished by the principles upon which its practice is based. These principles are continually reexamined in the light of scientific advances. The techniques of naturopathic medicine include modern and traditional, scientific and empirical methods."[2]

The philosophy of naturopathic medicine is embodied by the six principles of naturopathic practice that date back to the time of Hippocrates:

The Healing Power of Nature

Naturopathic physicians recognize an inherent ability of the body to heal itself. It is the role of the naturopathic physician to identify and remove obstacles to healing and recovery, and to facilitate and enhance this self-healing process.

Identify and Treat the Causes

Naturopathic physicians seek to remove the underlying causes of disease rather than merely eliminating or suppressing symptoms.

First Do No Harm

Naturopathic physicians strive to: 1) use methods that minimize harmful side effects, using the least force necessary to diagnose and treat, 2) prevent suppression of symptoms, and 3) acknowledge, respect, and work with each individual's self-healing process.

Doctor as Teacher

A primary role of naturopathic physicians is to educate and encourage individuals to take responsibility for their own health. They also recognize the therapeutic potential of the doctor/patient relationship.

Treat the Whole Person

Naturopathic physicians recognize that total health includes physical, mental, emotional, genetic, environmental, social, spiritual, and other factors. They encourage patients to pursue personal spiritual development.

Prevention

Naturopathic physicians encourage and emphasize disease prevention, i.e., assessing risk factors, heredity, and susceptibility to disease, and making appropriate interventions in partnership with patients to prevent illness. Naturopathic medicine is committed to creating a healthy world for humanity (American Association of Naturopathic Physicians, 1998).

Characteristics and Data

In 2000 the UCSF Center for the Health Professions reported that there were 1978 licensed naturopathic physicians practicing in North America. Since then, the profession more than doubled to 4010 in 2006.[3]

Most naturopathic doctors provide primary care natural medicine through office-based private practice. In states where NDs have been licensed for many years, they often work in collaboration with medical doctors or other healthcare professionals, and routinely refer patients for optimum management of a patient's health care, especially for those patients with severe, recalcitrant, or life-threatening conditions.

According to the *Chronicle of Higher Education's* Occupational Brief,[4] naturopathic physicians work 30 to 50 hours a week. Some practitioners see patients evenings or weekends. A few make house calls. Many naturopathic physicians spend time outside of office hours studying their patients' symptoms and reading journals. Many travel to lecture or teach. Naturopathic physicians who practice naturopathic obstetrics must be available at any time for births.

Earnings vary with the location of the practice, overhead, and whether insurance pays for treatment. While naturopathic physicians just starting out may typically earn $35,000 a year, some new graduates are challenged to create a living if they are not strong entrepreneurs. Experienced naturopathic physicians may earn from $45,000 to $100,000 a year. A few may earn $200,000 a year. Earnings also vary with professional certification or licensure, services offered, the emphasis of treatment, and the population where the practice is centered.

Clinical Care

Approach to patient care

Using the six principles outlined above, naturopathic physicians seek to understand the underlying and contributing factors in a patient's condition, remove obstacles to healing, strengthen or support the patient's inherent healing ability, and teach the patient how to prevent recurrence of the condition. For example, a child with recurrent otitis media is conventionally treated with repeated courses of antibiotics and, in some cases, tympanostomy and ear tubes. A naturopathic physician would use the history, physical examination, and laboratory tests to diagnose conditions that increase the child's susceptibility to becoming sick. These could include environmental allergies (dust mites, dander, etc.), food sensitivities (dairy, wheat, and eggs are often implicated), a diet high in simple carbohydrates (processed sugars), mechanical misalignments of the cervical spine or cranial bones, and sometimes emotional stress. Children routinely improve by addressing these factors, together with nutritional support and other naturopathic therapies.

In striving to attain an in-depth understanding of the patient's health, naturopathic physicians consider the combination of genetic predispositions with superimposed factors such as nutritional status, work and emotional stress, environmental allergens and toxins, and bio-mechanical data such as gait and posture.

Essential to a comprehensive evaluation is the extended interview, which ranges from 60–90 minutes for new patients. Typical follow-up visits range from 30 to 60 minutes. A standard review of systems is supplemented with patient-generated reports of daily activities, such as dietary habits, physical activity, and psychological issues. Naturopathic physicians perform physical examinations appropriate to the patient's presenting complaint and health history, and employ conventional laboratory and diagnostic imaging services as needed. Clinical evaluation is patient-centered and addresses a full range of factors that influence health as well as illness, generating a problem-oriented patient record.[5]

With many treatment options at their disposal, naturopathic physicians follow a distinct clinical thought process to individualize patient care according to naturopathic principles. In 1996 the AANP recommended that further work on practice principles move to the academic community. Clinical faculty and practitioners built on the core foundation throughout the 1990s.

In 1997, "The Process of Healing, a Unifying Theory of Naturopathic Medicine" was published in the *Journal of Naturopathic Medicine* (Zeff).[6] In 2006, "A Hierarchy of Healing: The Therapeutic Order" (Zeff, Snider, and Myers) was published in the *Textbook of Natural Medicine* (Pizzorno and Murray eds.).[7] The article and chapter presented three principles underlying the practice of naturopathic medicine. The first of these is the characterization of disease as a process rather than a pathologic entity. The second is the focus on the determinants of health rather than on pathology. The third is the concept of a therapeutic hierarchy. As taught in naturopathic medical schools, the therapeutic hierarchy is a guideline to applying the modalities of naturopathic medicine according to the unique needs of an individual patient, and the natural order of the healing process. The therapeutic hierarchy proposes the following order:

- Establish the conditions for health
- Stimulate the self-healing mechanisms (*vis medicatrix naturae*)
- Support weakened or damaged systems or organs
- Address structural integrity
- Address pathology using specific natural substances, modalities, or interventions
- Address pathology using specific pharmacologic or synthetic substances
- Suppress pathology

Let's return to our example of a child with recurrent otitis media, a common reason for seeking naturopathic care. Using the hierarchy above, a typical naturopathic approach to care would follow this protocol:

1. Look for and remove or address obstacles to health, such as allergies, environmental irritants (e.g., secondhand cigarette smoke), or a diet high in simple sugars.
2. Stimulate the healing power of nature with therapies like homeopathy and hydrotherapy.
3. Strengthen affected systems by providing immune support with vitamins C and A or oligopolysaccharides.
4. Address structural factors with soft tissue manual therapy like lymphatic drainage.

5. Treat the pathology with specific natural therapies such as topical garlic or hypericum oil.
6. Children typically respond well to the naturopathic approach outlined in the five preceding steps, experiencing fewer infections with faster recovery. However, should a child experience a particularly severe ear infection, or if there are other compromising factors, it may be necessary to prescribe a course of antibiotics.
7. If the infection still does not subside, referral to an MD may be necessary.

The therapeutic hierarchy creates a guideline for prescribing (or referring for) therapeutic life changes, homeopathic and botanical medicines, nutritional supplements, hydrotherapy, physical medicine, natural hygiene, manipulative therapy, and prescription drugs by naturopathic doctors that is both consistent with the profession's principles and addresses the patient's dynamic needs.[8]

Scope of practice

Every jurisdiction that licenses/regulates naturopathic medicine gives naturopathic physicians the authority to diagnose and treat. This includes the ability to take a health history, perform a physical examination, and order laboratory tests and diagnostic imaging. Prescribing privileges for each state vary greatly. A brief summary of statutory variations in scope of practice is given below, although scope in the licensed states generally reflects what is taught at accredited naturopathic medical schools. Naturopathic physicians are trained as primary care givers. Some NDs may choose to specialize in populations, modalities, or other focused areas of clinical practice as well.

- Arizona has the broadest ND prescribing privileges in the nation. Arizona NDs are allowed to independently prescribe all classes of prescription drugs, with exceptions for IV medicines (vitamins, minerals, and emergency resuscitation medications are permitted), chemotherapy drugs, and anti-psychotics.
- California currently allows NDs to prescribe drugs under the supervision of an MD or DO, and to prescribe hormones and epinephrine independently.
- Hawaii state law authorizes NDs to prescribe vitamins, minerals, amino acids, and fatty acids.

- Idaho passed a bill in 2005 authorizing licensure of NDs. The bill creates a formulary council to establish a formulary for use by NDs that is consistent with the training and education of NDs. The formulary will be reviewed on an annual basis. To date, the formulary has not been completed.
- Kansas passed an ND licensing law in 2003. It authorizes an intravenous and intramuscular formulary which must be under the supervision of a physician. Kansas and California require continuous MD supervision for prescribing.
- Maine NDs are allowed to independently prescribe non-controlled legend drugs after completing a 12-month collaborative relationship with a licensed allopathic or osteopathic physician to review the ND's prescribing practices.
- Montana law requires a five-member formulary committee to establish a natural substance formulary list and review the list on an annual basis. Among other items, the approved list of natural substances contains antibiotics and hormones.
- Oregon NDs have broad prescribing authority. All substances on the formulary are recommended by the formulary council and approved by the State Board of Naturopathic Examiners.
- Utah NDs are allowed to prescribe non-controlled drugs that are consistent with the competent practice of naturopathic medicine and are approved in collaboration with the Naturopathic Formulary Advisory Peer Committee.
- Vermont law authorizes the Commissioner of Health to establish the formulary with the advice of advisory appointees. The formulary lists the substances that are authorized as well as their route of administration, and in some instances, even the specific dose and length of treatment.
- Washington state law was amended in 2005 to allow NDs a broader formulary. HB 1546 defined naturopathic medicines to mean "vitamins; minerals; botanical medicines; homeopathic medicines; hormones; and those legend drugs and controlled substances consistent with naturopathic medical practice in accordance with rules established by the secretary." An updated formulary has not yet been completed.[6]

Referral practices

Naturopathic doctors (NDs) are trained and serve as primary care providers, an area of great current and future demand. NDs cooperate with all other health professions and refer patients to other practitioners and specialists for diagnosis or treatment when appropriate.[9]

Third-party payers

Insurance reimbursement for naturopathic physicians in the US varies from jurisdiction to jurisdiction, although in the regulated states many private and governmental programs cover ND care. In Canada, reimbursement also varies from province to province, but minimal coverage is generally available from the provincial health-care programs. Unfortunately, restrictions on fees and numbers of visits permitted drive most NDs out of provincial healthcare programs. Private insurance companies in Canada are beginning to offer more reasonable coverage, but most of the population doesn't have private insurance.

Integration Activities

Naturopathic physicians practice in a wide variety of clinical settings and collaborate with diverse practitioners from both conventional and alternative health professions. The following are 12 examples of innovative and integrative practices:

- Integrative Dermatology: A naturopathic physician and a board certified dermatologist (MD) practice, teach, and write together on combining the best of allopathic and naturopathic medicine.
- Pain: An anesthesiologist specializing in pain medicine brought two naturopathic physicians into his practice to help address his patients' needs more holistically.
- Community Health: At Community Health Centers of King County, Washington, two naturopathic doctors work as primary care providers, co-managing patients with the medical staff.[10]
- Native American Health: The San Carlos Apache Tribe hired a naturopathic physician as medical director for their Diabetes Prevention Program/Weight Management Clinic. The Clinic opened in September 2006.[11]

- Mental Health: In 2003, the Mental Health Center of Greater Manchester (New Hampshire's largest city) began integrating naturopathic medicine with other conventional psychiatric approaches.[12]
- Holistic Health: In North Carolina, a naturopathic physician brought together seven other practitioners—three massage therapists, a colon hydrotherapist, a second naturopathic physician, a counselor, and a hypnotherapist—to create a well-rounded holistic health center.
- Medical Mission: Mission of Mercy is a mobile medical center that treats thousands of Arizona's poorest. Since 2005, the medical director has been a naturopathic physician.[13]
- Naturopathic Urgent Care: At Centro de Salud Familiar, located in an economically challenged neighborhood, naturopathic physicians may treat 50 or more patients a day for a wide range of acute, traumatic, and serious chronic conditions.
- Integrative Rheumatology: Many patients suffering from autoimmune diseases like rheumatoid arthritis and systemic lupus erythematosus benefit by combining the skills and knowledge of a conventional rheumatologist (MD) and a naturopathic physician.
- Integrative Oncology: Cancer Treatment Centers of America integrates naturopathic medicine into its hospital and outpatient centers, providing patients a wide range of treatment options and expertise in combating their illness.
- Public, Rural, and Community Health: In proximity to naturopathic colleges, public and community health clinics often integrate services from naturopathic physicians. Washington State provides student loan forgiveness to naturopathic physicians for service to urban and rural underserved communities and includes naturopathic physicians as primary care providers in its medical home legislation. Vermont provides Medicaid coverage for naturopathic care.
- International healthcare services for communities in need (Nicaragua, Mexico, Africa, India are examples) are growing in naturopathic medicine through college-based student preceptorships and internships offered by organizations such as Naturopathic Doctors International.

Education

Schools and Programs

Acceptance into a naturopathic medical school requires extensive pre-medical course work and a bachelor's degree. Pre-medical coursework includes biology, general and organic chemistry, physics, psychology, and humanities. The admission process requires official undergraduate transcripts and essays providing insights into the candidate's understanding of naturopathic medicine and motivation for applying to naturopathic medical school. Those individuals who meet the application criteria are interviewed by faculty, students, and staff to assess academic ability, interpersonal skills, and professional demeanor.

There are currently approximately 1978 students enrolled in six accredited or pre-accredited naturopathic medical schools in North America. The mean cumulative GPA for admitted students is 3.30, and the mean science GPA is 3.46. The average age of students enrolled in the Fall 2006 entering class was 31, with a bi-modal distribution of students in their early 20s right out of undergraduate school, and older students pursuing a second (or third) career. The typical naturopathic student population is composed of approximately 70% women and 30% men. Under-represented minority students comprise approximately 20% of the entering class.

Matriculation at each school begins with an extensive orientation program aimed at preparing students for the rigorous academic and clinical challenges that lie ahead. Students often describe their four years of naturopathic medical education as a personally transformative experience on intellectual, emotional, and sometimes spiritual levels. Hours of study lead to frustrations and revelations. Relationships with classmates turn into lifelong friendships. And patient encounters can at times provide transcendent moments with people engaged in the healing process.

Curriculum content

Naturopathic medical education integrates the biomedical sciences, Western diagnostic decision-making skills, and natural and conventional therapies. Students spend over 4000 hours during the four-year post baccalaureate program learning the art and science of naturopathic medicine. Naturopathic principles, philosophy, and theory guide the curriculum and provide a conceptual framework from which students develop a profound understanding of humans in health and disease.

In 2005 the Association of Accredited Naturopathic Medical Colleges set in motion a two-year project to define core competencies common to all schools. The academic deans, chief academic and clinical officers, and experts from within and outside the profession met at schools in the US and Canada to profile a graduate of a naturopathic medical school. The report, published in 2007, delineated knowledge, skills, and attitudes organized around five key roles:[14]

- The medical expert—who integrates naturopathic principles and philosophy to reach accurate diagnoses and formulate safe, effective treatment plans, manage patient care, and interact with other healthcare professionals for patients' benefit.
- The naturopathic manager—who can create, develop, and maintain a clinical practice. Courses in practice management, ethics, and jurisprudence join clinical training to provide students with the necessary experience and knowledge to succeed in this endeavor.
- The naturopathic professional—well grounded in the history of the profession, who understands the importance of ethical practice, public health, and participation in professional affairs on a state and national level.
- The naturopathic health scholar—who practices *docere*, the role of doctor as teacher, with individual patients and in the wider community; who stays current through continuing medical education and reading; and who critically evaluates the peer-reviewed literature.
- The naturopathic health advocate—who practices prevention with patients, understands and promotes the relationship of environmental sustainability to human health, and participates in the broader healthcare dialog.

The curriculum is dynamic, adapting to meet the changing healthcare needs of a population under stress from poor dietary habits, sedentary lifestyles, and environmental toxins. Naturopathic medical education pays particular attention to the growing epidemic of chronic diseases affecting every age group and societal sector. Courses in *year one* focus on developing students' understanding of the human body in health and disease. Anatomy, biochemistry, microbiology, physiology, embryology, histology, neuroanatomy, and genetics accompany introductory classes in naturopathic philosophy, nutrition, mind-body medicine, homeopathy, and botanical medicine. The *second year* introduces students to Western diagnostic knowledge, with courses in clinical diagnosis, pathology, lab diagnosis, and diagnostic imaging. Students gain critical history and physical exam skills in lab sections and study labs. Intermediate courses in naturopathic therapeutics continue to deepen students' understanding of clinical nutrition, manipulative therapy and physical medicine, acupuncture, homeopathy, and botanical medicine. In years *three and four*, students engage in supervised patient care on diverse clinical rotations. Didactic education continues to build expertise in naturopathic therapeutics and adds in-depth coursework in pediatrics, gynecology, gastroenterology, orthopedics, cardiovascular health, disorders of the eyes, ears, nose and throat, nephrology, and dermatology. Naturopathic principles guide the curriculum design and course content.

Clinical training, the heart of naturopathic medical education, takes place in a variety of clinical settings. Clinical faculty provide training, supervision, and care in multidisciplinary medical centers that provide outpatient care to patients and clinical education to students. Students see patients with a wide range of clinical conditions, from acute illnesses (e.g., respiratory infections, influenza, gastrointestinal infections and infestations, musculoskeletal injuries, and minor lacerations) to chronic, sometimes life-threatening diseases (e.g., asthma, diabetes, colitis, heart disease, hypertension, hyperlipidemia, metabolic syndrome, cancer, kidney disease, eczema and other skin conditions). Experienced licensed clinicians, including naturopathic doctors, medical doctors, osteopaths, chiropractors, acupuncturists, and psychologists supervise students and oversee quality patient care.

In addition to the colleges' outpatient clinics and medical centers, each school provides free care to thousands of medically underserved women, children, and men. Students work with patients at homeless shelters, HIV/AIDS clinics, drug and alcohol rehabilitation programs, elementary schools in impoverished immigrant communities, shelters for battered women and children, and community health centers. These programs benefit the patients, who receive high quality naturopathic, conventional, and preventive care, and the students, who are introduced to a very diverse patient population often suffering disproportionately from both chronic and acute conditions. Students rank these clinical encounters among the most important and transformative experiences in their academic careers.

Faculty at naturopathic medical schools must have terminal degrees in their respective fields. Faculty in the biomedical sciences predominantly have PhDs; the clinical sciences are taught by naturopathic doctors and other licensed practitioners such as medical doctors, osteopathic doctors, chiropractors, psychologists, and acupuncturists.

Naturopathic medical schools develop healers with knowledge, discrimination, and sensitivity. The demands on the student are great, but so also are the rewards. Learning within a healing environment is challenging, inspiring, and sustaining.

Accreditation

Founded in 1978, the Council on Naturopathic Medical Education (CNME) incorporated in the District of Columbia to accredit naturopathic medical schools in the US and Canada. A member of the Association of Specialized and Professional Accreditors, the CNME is the sole naturopathic accrediting body recognized by the US Department of Education. The CNME board comprises institutional members from accredited naturopathic medical schools, profession members who are licensed naturopathic physicians, and public members who possess educational experience and are unaffiliated with any naturopathic program or the profession. In addition to establishing educational criteria for accreditation, the CNME requires institutions to participate in the self-study process. Site visits are conducted for candidacy, for initial accreditation, and to renew accreditation.[15]

In addition to programmatic accreditation by the CNME, all naturopathic medical schools in the United States have institutional accreditation from their respective regional accrediting agencies, and in Canada from their provincial accrediting bodies. Accreditation holds institutions to high academic, financial, and human resource standards. Faculty are required to have terminal degrees in their chosen fields (PhD for the basic sciences; ND, MD, DO, or DC for clinical sciences). Accreditation also ensures that schools respect academic freedom in teaching and include faculty, staff, and students in decision-making processes. Equally important, accredited institutions join a community of colleges and universities who share the ideas, innovations, and experiences that drive continuous quality improvement.

There are currently seven naturopathic medical schools recognized by CNME. All are accredited except the program at National University of Health Sciences where the naturopathic medical program has been accepted as a candidate for accreditation.

Institution	Location	Founded
Bastyr University	Seattle, Washington	1978
Boucher Institute of Naturopathic Medicine	Vancouver, British Columbia	1998
Canadian College of Naturopathic Medicine	Toronto, Ontario	1978
National College of Natural Medicine	Portland, Oregon	1956
National University of Health Sciences	Lombard, Illinois	2004
Southwest College of Naturopathic Medicine	Tempe, Arizona	1992
University of Bridgeport College of Naturopathic Medicine	Bridgeport, Connecticut	1997

Regulation and Certification

Regulatory status

Naturopathic medicine is licensed/regulated in 15 states (Alaska, Arizona, California, Connecticut, Idaho, Hawaii, Kansas, Maine, Minnesota, Montana, New Hampshire, Oregon, Utah, Vermont, and Washington), the District of Columbia, Puerto Rico, and the Virgin Islands. Licensure efforts are underway in at least 12 other states. In Canada, NDs are licensed/regulated in four provinces (British Columbia, Manitoba, Ontario and Saskatchewan) and legislation in Alberta is in process. Supporting the regulatory process is a high priority for both the American Association of Naturopathic Physicians and the Canadian Association of Naturopathic Doctors. To be eligible to be licensed as a naturopathic physician in a regulated jurisdiction, one must graduate from an accredited or pre-accredited naturopathic medical school.

Board examinations

All jurisdictions that license/regulate naturopathic medicine require physicians to pass a licensing examination. The Board Examination developed by the Naturopathic Physicians Licensing

Examinations (NPLEX) and administered by the North American Board of Naturopathic Examiners (NABNE) is given in two parts. Students take Part I Biomedical Science Examinations after completion of biomedical science training. Part II Clinical Sciences Examinations may be taken after graduation from a CNME-accredited naturopathic medical school.

NPLEX Part I—Biomedical Science Exam Areas
Anatomy
Biochemistry and Genetics
Microbiology and Immunology
Pathology
Physiology

NPLEX Part II—Core Exam Areas
Physical & Clinical Diagnosis
Laboratory Diagnosis & Diagnostic Imaging
Botanical Medicine
Clinical Nutrition
Physical Medicine
Homeopathy
Psychology
Emergency Medicine & Medical Procedures
Pharmacology

NPLEX Part II—Elective Exam Areas
Minor Surgery
Acupuncture

In 2007 NPLEX moved to an integrated case-based exam format for the Part II Core Clinical Science Examination. In August 2009, the first integrated case-based Part I Biomedical Science Examination was administered.

Research

Clinical trials and some laboratory studies are conducted at naturopathic medical schools in the US and Canada. As the profession matures, the number and quality of research studies improve. Studies have been published, for example, on the effectiveness of individual botanical medicines—stinging nettles for hay fever, echinacea for colds, black cohosh for menopausal symptoms; homeopathic medicines—coca for altitude sickness, regional pollens for hay fever; naturopathic detoxification for environmental illnesses; nutritional supplementation—SAMe for osteoarthritis; and naturopathic approaches to diabetes.

The National Institutes of Health National Center for Complementary and Alternative Medicine funded the development of the Naturopathic Medical Research Agenda (NMRA) from 2002–2004. The NMRA brought together naturopathic physicians and conventional research scientists to identify and prioritize a list of research questions and areas.[16] The research departments at every naturopathic medical school participated in a series of meetings and produced a consensus document on the future of naturopathic research. The highest priorities focused on three areas:

- Naturopathic treatment of type 2 diabetes
- Naturopathic care for the preservation and promotion of optimal health in geriatric populations
- Developing methodologies to understand the healing process

Challenges and Opportunities

Key challenges 2009–2012

The greatest challenge facing the naturopathic profession today is having enough practitioners to meet the growing demand for this kind of health care. Although the number of naturopathic medical schools is increasing, there are fewer than 5,000 naturopathic physicians in practice today. Unless this number grows substantially in the next decade, other professions will adopt and adapt naturopathic practices to meet the public's health needs.

- Currently less than a third of states regulate naturopathic medicine. The profession must continue to push for licensure for the profession to maximally impact healthcare.
- Confusion among consumers exists about the differences between CAM professionals and nonprofessionals—who does what and what is their training?
- Expansion of scope of practice lags behind in some jurisdictions.

Key opportunities 2009–2012

The naturopathic profession's greatest strength lies in meeting the growing need for health care in general, and for safe, effective natural care in particular. The emerging epidemic of chronic diseases traceable to diet, environment, and lifestyle (e.g., diabetes, hypertension, heart disease, gastrointestinal disorders, environmental illnesses, allergies, cognitive and developmental disorders in children) is emphasizing the need for patients to accept responsibility for their health and to partner with physicians who can assist them on this journey. Consequently, naturopathic physicians are in greater demand than ever before.

Today, graduates find diverse practice opportunities that were unheard of twenty years ago. In addition to solo practice, naturopathic physicians increasingly work in clinical settings with medical and osteopathic doctors, chiropractors, acupuncturists, massage therapists, and other CAM practitioners; in tribal clinics on Native American lands; in public health clinics; at resorts and spas; in mental health clinics; in substance abuse programs; and in corporate wellness programs. Opportunities for the next few years include:

- The number of naturopathic medical schools more than doubled in the past 20 years and others are being planned.
- A larger and better qualified applicant pool is available to the schools.
- Graduating class sizes have been increasing.
- The number of conventional medical students pursuing primary care/family care has been decreasing (down to 24% in Canada), leaving a void which NDs can help fill.
- Competencies and outcomes have been clearly defined for accredited schools and are regularly updated as the profession develops.
- Collaboration is increasing among schools and other professional ND organizations for the growth and betterment of the profession and the patients we serve.

Resources

Organizations and websites
- American Association of Naturopathic Midwives
  www.naturopathicmidwives.org

- American Association of Naturopathic Physicians
  www.naturopathic.org
- Association of Accredited Naturopathic Medical Colleges
  www.aanmc.org
- Bastyr University
  www.bastyr.edu
- Boucher Institute of Naturopathic Medicine
  www.binm.org
- Canadian Association of Naturopathic Doctors
  www.cand.ca (also www.naturopathicassoc.ca)
- Canadian College of Naturopathic Medicine
  www.ccnm.edu
- Council on Naturopathic Medical Education
  www.cnme.org
- Homeopathic Academy of Naturopathic Physicians
  www.hanp.net
- National College of Natural Medicine
  www.ncnm.edu
- National University of the Health Sciences
  www.nuhs.edu
- Natural Doctors International
  www.ndimed.org
- Naturopathic Academy of Therapeutic Injection
  www.injectiontx.org
- Naturopathic Medical Student Association
  www.naturopathicstudent.org
- Oncology Association of Naturopathic Physicians
  www.oncanp.org
- Southwest College of Naturopathic Medicine
  www.scnm.edu
- University of Bridgeport College of Naturopathic Medicine
  www.bridgeport.edu/naturopathy

Citations

1. Hough H, Dower C, O'Nell E. *Profile of a Profession: Naturopathic Practice.* San Francisco, CA: University of California at San Francisco Center for the Health Professions; 2001.
2. American Association of Naturopathic Physicians. Select Committee on the Definition of Naturopathic Medicine, Snider P, Zeff J, co-chairs. Definition of Naturopathic Medicine. Position Paper. Rippling River, OR; 1989.

3. Albert D, Martinez D. The supply of naturopathic physicians in the United States and Canada continues to increase. *Comp Health Prac Rev.* 2006;11(2):120-122.
4. Chronicle Guidance Publications. Occupational Brief 624: Naturopathic Physicians. http://www.chronicleguidance.com/store.asp?pid=7330. Accessed November 17, 2009.
5. Dunne N, Benda W, Kim L, et al. Naturopathic medicine: what can patients expect? *J Fam Pract.* 2005;54(12).
6. Zeff J. The process of healing: a unifying theory of naturopathic medicine. *J Naturopathic Med.* 1977;7(1):122-125.
7. Zeff J , Snider P, Myers S. A hierarchy of healing: the therapeutic order. The unifying theory of naturopathic medicine. In: Pizzorno JE, Murray MT. *Textbook of Natural Medicine.* Vol 1. 3rd ed. Philadelphia, PA: Elsevier; 2006:27-40.
8. Findings and Recommendations Regarding the Prescribing and Furnishing Authority of a Naturopathic Doctor. Bureau of Naturopathic Medicine; January 2007.
9. *Health Professions Advisors Guide.* Champaign, IL: National Association of Advisors for the Health Professions Inc; 2007.
10. Community Health Centers of King County, Washington. HealthPoint Web site. http://www.healthpointchc.org/. Accessed November 17, 2009.
11. AANMCInformationalForum.http://www.aanmc.org/careers/alumni-leaders-in-the-field/andrew-j-kaufmann.php. Accessed November 17, 2009.
12. Sager J, Potenza D, Oxendine MB, Guilemette M. Integration of Naturopathic Medicine in a Traditional Behavioral Health System. The Mental Health Center of Greater Manchester Web site. http://www.mhcgm. org/pdf/Integration%20Manual%20Sept%202006.pdf. September 2006. Accessed November 17, 2009.
13. Mission of Mercy Website. http://www.amissionofmercy.org. Accessed November 17, 2009.
14. Professional Competency Profile. Association of Accredited Naturopathic Medical Colleges. www.aanmc.org.
15. US Department of Education Office of Postsecondary Education. http://www.ed.gov/admins/finaid/accred/index.html. Accessed November 17, 2009.
16. Standish L, Calabrese C, Snider P. The naturopathic medical research agenda: the future and foundation of naturopathic medical science. *J Altern Complement Med.* 2006;12(3):341-345.

Bibliography
General Naturopathic Medicine

Alschuler LN, Gazella KA. *Alternative Medicine Magazine's Definitive Guide to Cancer: An Integrative Approach to Prevention, Treatment, and Healing.* Berkeley, CA: Celestial Arts; 2007.
Bove M. *An Encyclopedia of Natural Healing for Children and Infants.* New York, NY: McGraw-Hill; 2001.

Canadian College of Naturopathic Medicine Press. Fifteen textbooks based on naturopathic curriculum, written by naturopathic physicians, faculty, and lecturers. http://www.ccnmpress.com/. Accessed November 17, 2009.

Hudson T. *Women's Encyclopedia of Natural Medicine: Alternative Therapies and Integrative Medicine.* Lincolnwood, IL: Keats; 1999.

Pizzorno JE, Murray MT, Joiner-Bey H. *The Clinician's Handbook of Natural Medicine.* 2nd ed. Philadelphia, PA: Churchill Livingston; 2002.

Pizzorno JE, Murray MT. *The Encyclopedia of Natural Medicine.* 2nd ed, revised. Roseville, CA: Prima Publishing; 1997.

Pizzorno JE, Murray MT. *The Textbook of Natural Medicine.* 3rd ed. Philadelphia, PA: Elsevier; 2006.

Pizzorno JE. *Total Wellness: Improve Your Health by Understanding the Body's Healing Systems.* Roseville, CA: Prima Publishing; 1997.

Standish L, Calabrese C, Snider P. *The Future and Foundations of Naturopathic Medical Research Science: Naturopathic Medical Research Agenda.* Kenmore, WA: Bastyr University Press; 2005.

Yarnell E. *Naturopathic Gastroenterology.* East Wenatchee, WA: Healing Mountain Publishing Inc; 2000.

Naturopathic Philosophy

Boyle W, Saine A. *Lectures in Naturopathic Hydrotherapy.* East Palestine, OH: Buckeye Naturopathic Press; 1988.

Kirchfeld F, Boyle W. *Nature Doctors: Pioneers in Naturopathic Medicine.* Portland, OR: Medicina Biologica; 1994.

Kneipp S. *My Water-Cure.* New ed. Champaign, IL: Standard Publications Inc; 2007.

Lindlahr H. *Nature Cure.* Charleston, SC: BiblioBazaar LLC; 2007.

Lindlahr H. *Philosophy of Natural Therapeutics.* Champaign, IL: Standard Publications Inc; 2007.

Lust B. *Collected Works of Dr. Benedict Lust.* East Wenatchee, WA: Healing Mountain Publishing Inc; 2006.

Smith F. *An Introduction to Principles and Practice of Naturopathic Medicine.* Toronto, Ontario, Canada: CCNM Press; 2008.

Zeff JL. The process of healing: a unifying theory of naturopathic medicine. *J Naturopathic Med.* 1997;7(1):122-5.

Zeff J , Snider P, Myers S. A hierarchy of healing: the therapeutic order. The unifying theory of naturopathic medicine. In: Pizzorno JE, Murray MT. *Textbook of Natural Medicine.* Vol 1. 3rd ed. Philadelphia, PA: Elsevier; 2006:27-40.

Other

Chaitow L, Blake E, Orrock P, Wallden M, Snider P, Zeff J. *Naturopathic Physical Medicine: Theory and Practice For Manual Therapists and Naturopaths.* Philadelphia, PA: Churchill Livingston Elsevier; 2008.

Dooley TR. *Homeopathy Beyond Flat Earth Medicine.* 2nd ed. San Diego, CA: Timing Publications; 2002.

Marz RB. *Medical Nutrition from Marz.* Portland, OR: Quiet Lion Press; 1997.

Mitchell W. *Plant Medicine in Practice: Using the Teachings of John Bastyr.* Philadelphia, PA: Churchill Livingston Publishing; 2003.

Murray M, Pizzorno J, Pizzorno L. *The Condensed Encyclopedia of Healing Foods.* New York, NY: Atria Books; 2006.

Neustadt J. *A Revolution in Health through Nutritional Biochemistry.* Bloomington, IN: iUniverse, Inc; 2007.

Stargrove M, Treasure J, McKee DL. *Herb, Nutrient, and Drug Interactions: Clinical Implications and Therapeutic Strategies.* St. Louis, MO: Mosby; 2007.

Tilgner S. *Herbal Medicine from the Heart of the Earth.* Pleasant Hill, OR: Wise Acres; 1999.

Journals and Periodicals

International Journal of Naturopathic Medicine. http://www.intjnm.org. Peer-reviewed online journal.

Naturopathic Doctor News and Review. http://www.ndnr.com. Professional news and information resource for naturopathic physicians in North America.

Appendices

Related Integrative Practice Fields

Ayurvedic Medicine

Holistic Medicine

Holistic Nursing

Homeopathy

Integrative Medicine

Yoga Therapy

Ayurvedic Medicine

Felicia Marie Tomasko, RN

Partner Organization: National Ayurvedic Medical Association

About the Author: Tomasko is an Ayurvedic professional and a member of the board of directors of the National Ayurvedic Medical Association, a member of the board of directors of the California Association of Ayurvedic Medicine, and the editor in chief of *LA YOGA Ayurveda and Health* magazine.

Philosophy, Mission, and Goals

While the practice of Ayurveda as a system of medicine is in its relative infancy in the US as far as education, regulation, recognition, scope, and numbers of people practicing are concerned, it has a long historical tradition in its native cultures, originating from the Indian subcontinent.

A translation of the Sanskrit word Ayurveda is "science of life." This science includes eight branches, as outlined in the written textual tradition. The written texts of Ayurveda are variously dated, depending on the source and scholarship. Three primary texts are the Charaka Samhita (the most recent agreed-upon date for this text is at the beginning of the common era, but many sources suggest it is older, or at least a compilation of an ancient oral tradition), the Sushruta Samhita, and Vagbhata's Ashtanga Hridaya Samhita. Generally, information included therein is considered to be the genesis of classical Ayurveda. Other texts add to the body of knowledge. Over its history, the practices and therapies of Ayurveda have evolved.

In general, Ayurveda is concerned with an individual's relationship with his/her own body, mind, and spirit, as well as with the natural world. The framework in which this is understood consists of the five elements (earth, water, fire, air, and ether/space) and their combination into the three doshas: vata (air and ether/space), pitta (fire and water), and kapha (water and earth). These exist in the world around us as well as the world within us. Vata is characterized by the qualities of being light, dry, expansive, and changeable. Pitta is hot, intense, transformational, and sharp. Kapha is stable, heavy, solid, cold, oily, and light in color.

Many physiological processes are described as falling under the categories of these doshas. For example, movement in the body is governed by vata, digestion and transformation by pitta, and insulation and lubrication by kapha. According to Ayurveda, people have a unique constitutional makeup (prakruti), with individual proportionality of the doshas. Out of balance, disease is more likely to take hold; importance is placed on disease prevention and maintaining balance with the ever-changing forces of nature. Balance is not static, but is constantly shifting. Thus, individuals must adjust their practices, routines, and lifestyles as necessary to maintain balance. One example is the precept to adjust one's diet with the seasons, favoring seasonal foods and even modifying the amount of cooked versus raw foods. Ayurveda is not exclusive of modern medicine, and combines well philosophically and practically because of its inclusivity.

Characteristics and Data

The National Ayurvedic Medical Association (NAMA) launched a survey at the end of 2007 at one of the organization's annual conferences to determine the state of the profession: approximate numbers of people practicing, educational levels, and other data. In order to obtain a more comprehensive body of data, the survey was revised and launched again in 2009. The survey can be found on the NAMA website at: http://www.ayurveda-nama.org/survey.php.

Scope of Practice

Since Ayurveda is an unlicensed profession in the US as of this writing, scope of practice follows the traditional scope mentioned in the Ayurvedic texts, with modifications and limitations necessitated by practitioner training currently available in this country and the legal scopes of practice of other healthcare professions in the US. For example, the Susruta Samhita outlines some surgical techniques which are not performed by Ayurvedic doctors or practitioners in the US. Ayurvedic practitioners who have completed different tiers of training practice different techniques. For example, panchakarma (a Sanskrit word that means five actions) is a group of cleansing techniques used in Ayurveda. Some people are trained to recommend only, others to be hands-on therapists, while others are more highly-trained practitioners who actually supervise the program.

Integration Activities

Many Ayurvedic professionals who are members of the National Ayurvedic Medical Association are also licensed healthcare providers in fields such as medicine, midwifery, chiropractic, nursing, massage therapy, and physical therapy. Because of this, increasing collaboration is occurring in research settings, clinics, and hospitals. A number of Ayurvedic professionals are also yoga teachers and/or yoga therapists, and introductory concepts of Ayurveda are increasingly taught in yoga teacher training programs and yoga therapy training courses.

Education

Ayurveda initially became visible in the US largely (but not exclusively) through efforts of spiritual communities. In the 1970s, for example, the Transcendental Meditation® (TM) community brought doctors trained in India to the US to offer Ayurvedic consultations to meditators. Dr. Deepak Chopra is probably the most well-known person who rose to prominence initially from within the TM community. Other esteemed doctors, both Indian natives who came to the US to practice, as well as Westerners who completed extensive training in India, have furthered the dissemination of Ayurvedic teachings as well as the profession in the US.

People practicing Ayurveda in the US have varying educational backgrounds. Some have come from Indian private or governmental universities where they received a BAMS degree (bachelor of Ayurvedic medical science), an MASc (master's in Ayurvedic science), or, more recently, an MD Ayurved (medical doctor of Ayurveda).

Additionally, training programs in the US, Europe, and even India exist outside the Indian system of medical education. Courses include intensives, weekend programs, certificate courses, and master's level and clinical doctorate programs, of which all currently enroll and graduate students in the US. In addition to Western-style academic programs, some modern Ayurvedic programs feature intensive internship or apprenticeship components, traditionally known as gurukula studies. These actively accept students in post-graduate models. So far, 30 schools in the United States, with a variety of programs, have been working with NAMA to develop educational standards.

Regulation and Certification

While Ayurveda is currently a licensed medical profession in its native India, as well as in other countries such as Nepal and Sri Lanka, the practice of Ayurveda is currently not licensed or otherwise regulated (other than self-regulation within the community) in the United States. Professional organizations, such as the National Ayurvedic Medical Association (NAMA), are developing educational standards, drafting reasonable scope of practice guidelines, and discussing a certification exam.

Research

The TM community sponsors hundreds of scientific studies investigating meditation as well as Ayurvedic practices; yet, as funding increases for CAM-related disciplines, Ayurveda still remains behind other systems in study numbers. One challenge is that the nature of Ayurveda does not easily lend itself to the most common types of studies used in the scientific world today, as therapies are tailored to the individual rather than standardized for a particular condition. Still, many therapies, herbal remedies, and other techniques utilized have been and continue to be studied with positive results, including turmeric (*Curcuma longa*) for varied uses including diabetes management, inflammation and joint health, and bitter gourd (*Momordica charantia*) for diabetes prevention and treatment.

Challenges and Opportunities

Key challenges 2009–2012

Ayurveda is an old and venerated system of medicine that is not yet regulated in the US and is not widely known. Greater understanding and recognition of Ayurveda by the general public and the larger medical community are some of this profession's most significant current challenges. Other challenges include:

- Identification of Ayurvedic practitioners at all levels currently active in the US
- Unification of a dispersed and diverse community
- Development of clear educational standards that take into account differing training methodologies and lineages within Ayurveda
- Identification of agreed-upon scope of practice that both stays true to Ayurveda's long historical tradition and is relevant in modern integrated healthcare practice
- Strengthening educational programs to train practitioners to work with other healthcare providers
- Development and dissemination of research priorities and methodologies
- Communication with different Ayurvedic communities worldwide to develop common goals in furthering the profession
- Work with the Ayurvedic herbal community to support sustainability in obtaining farmed or gathered herbs as well as supporting appropriately labeled and safe imported herbal supplies

Key opportunities 2009–2012

Ayurveda offers a sophisticated, individualized system of lifestyle and rejuvenation practices, stress reduction techniques, and dietary recommendations to support the process of finding balance and achieving optimum health. These practices can contribute to making a positive difference in the modern healthcare system. Opportunities in the coming years involve allowing these practices to become more widely accessible by working directly with the general public and through interfacing and collaborating with other healthcare professionals and modalities. Other related opportunities include:

- Teaching tangible, low-cost, self-implemented techniques for health maintenance and possible prevention of the chronic illnesses so prevalent today

- Increased collaboration with other healthcare providers and professions for fully integrated healthcare models and systems to support preventive medicine and well-being
- Combining the philosophy and therapies of Ayurveda with other healthcare systems to address often recalcitrant chronic illnesses, many of which have lifestyle components
- Continued support of healthcare freedom legislation around the country as well as pursuing licensure for the profession
- Increased membership in NAMA as a means of networking and uniting the profession as it is practiced today
- Ongoing support for educational programs training people at all levels of the Ayurvedic progression

Organizations

The National Ayurvedic Medical Association is a 501(c)(6) organization and the largest Ayurvedic professional organization in the US (http://www.ayurveda-nama.org). Membership ranges between 350–450 active members, but it is unknown what percentage of the Ayurvedic community in the US this represents. People can join as a student, general, or professional member of NAMA. Professional members' credentials are reviewed by the organization before the member is accepted as such.

NAMA held its sixth annual conference in 2008; at the time of this writing, the seventh annual conference is scheduled for April, 2010 in the San Francisco area and the eighth annual conference is scheduled for April, 2011 in the mid-Atlantic region. These conferences are a means for members of the profession, students, and enthusiasts to come together.

Within NAMA, a council of schools has been actively meeting in person and via conference calls to discuss educational standards and scope of practice for practitioners. Some states, notably Washington and California, have active state organizations (Washington Ayurvedic Medical Association/WAMA and the California Association of Ayurvedic Medicine/CAAM, respectively). These organizations have been working in close collaboration with NAMA. One of the stated purposes of CAAM is to pursue licensure of Ayurvedic medicine within the state of California.

While NAMA may be the most visible nonpartisan organization of Ayurvedic practitioners, it does not necessarily represent everyone within the US Ayurvedic community.

- California Association of Ayurvedic Medicine (CAAM)
  www.ayurveda-caam.org/
- National Ayurvedic Medical Association (NAMA)
  www.ayurveda-nama.org/
- Washington Ayurvedic Medical Association (WAMA)
  www.ayurveda-wama.org/

Holistic Medicine

Hal Blatman, MD, Kjersten Gmeiner, MD, Donna Nowak, CH, CRT

Partner Organization: American Holistic Medical Association

About the Authors: Blatman is board president, Gmeiner previously served as a trustee, and Nowak is executive director for the American Holistic Medical Association.

Disclaimer: The information presented here is a portrait of the profession/discipline. It does not necessarily reflect endorsed statements of agreement by the profession or discipline portrayed.

Philosophy, Mission, and Goals

Holistic medicine is the art and science of healing that addresses care of the whole person—body, mind, and spirit. Since 1978, the AHMA has been helping transform conventional/allopathic medicine to a sustainable, more holistic model. The practice of holistic medicine integrates conventional health care with complementary and alternative medicine (CAM) therapies to promote optimal health and wellness as well as to prevent and treat disease.

Optimal health is the primary goal of holistic medical practice. It is the conscious pursuit of the highest level of functioning and balance of the physical, environmental, mental, emotional, social, and spiritual aspects of human experience, resulting in a dynamic state of being fully alive. Other principles include the healing power of love, treating the whole person, innate healing power in each one of us, integration of healing systems, relationship-centered care, individuality, prevention, teaching by example, and illness as an opportunity for growth and learning.

The AHMA serves as an advocate for the use of holistic and integrative medicine by all licensed healthcare providers. We are a home for collective voices for both those providing and those seeking more integrative healthcare.

Characteristics and Data

Holistic medicine in the US was conceived and practiced by medical doctors as early as the 1950s, building on the various complementary medical traditions of the US dating back to the mid-19th century. Currently, more than 1,000 physicians have been certified by the American Board of Integrative Holistic Medicine.

Scope of Practice

Scope of practice is defined by conventional medical licensing statutes and agencies in all 50 states. Three states, Arizona, Connecticut, and Nevada, have homeopathic medical boards for physicians practicing homeopathy and other complementary and alternative therapies.

Integration Activities

- Participation in cross-discipline dialogues such as the Summit in Humanistic Medicine and the National Education Dialogue to Advance Integrated Health Care
- Full voting membership in the AHMA includes MDs, DOs, and all licensed healthcare providers
- Collaborative conferences (e.g., American Holistic Nurses Association 2006, American Association of Naturopathic Physicians 2008, MetroHealth Hospital 2009)
- Development of new approaches for specialty complementary and integrative medicine education (including CME) as well as the development of local programming across the country
- AHMA Board representation from all categories of licensed healthcare providers who are members as well as other business specialties and the public.
- Enhancement of AHMA's website to support others who provide services in the field of integrative health care

Education

Most education in this area is obtained in the postgraduate arena. Most holistic physicians receive their graduate training in another field and then become boarded in holistic medicine. The American Board of Integrative Holistic Medicine (ABIHM) offers a board review course for physicians, using a defined, evidence-based curriculum. Conventional MD or DO training and licensing is the prerequisite for board certification in holistic medicine.

Many postgraduate fellowships are available in integrative medicine and a new residency in integrative medicine—Integrative Medicine in Residency (IMR) program—is currently being piloted in eight family practice residency programs. It is currently in year two of its curriculum. IMR is a required, in-depth competency-based curriculum that is integrated into a typical three-year family practice residency program. It utilizes a web-based curriculum, program-specific experiential exercises, and group process-oriented activities.

Regulation and Certification

Board certification has been available via examination through the American Board of Integrative Holistic Medicine since 1999. Visit www.holisticboard.org. Holistic medicine, homeopathy, and medical acupuncture board certification may affect insurance reimbursement and credentialing even though these board certifications, like all complementary therapies that offer board certification, are not yet recognized by the American Board of Medical Specialties.

Research

Currently, a broad spectrum of research is being done nationally and internationally on specific modalities and therapies. Studies of clinical sites practicing integrative/holistic medicine are underway to examine its impact. AHMA serves as a resource to individuals and organizations doing research on systems of practice.

Challenges and Opportunities

Key challenges 2009–2012
- Outcomes documentation for the system of holistic medicine as an effective intervention
- Advancing the principles of holism into the conventional medical model

- Maintaining economic stability of the organization and the field
- Providing equitable access for patients and practitioners alike
- Providing adequate educational opportunities
- Establishing legitimacy amid the current medical hierarchy
- Establishing clear definitions and practices within this rapidly evolving field

Key opportunities 2009–2012

Through an internal restructuring and major educational campaign, AHMA expects to continue to increase membership over the next three years. We are reaching out to conventional/allopathic physicians who are ready to incorporate new healthcare perspectives into their clinical work, and making it easier for them to partner with or refer to qualified CAM practitioners. Other opportunities include:

- Increasing the understanding and stability of the field of holistic medicine through the strengthening of interdisciplinary and inter-organizational relationships
- Increasing education of healthcare consumers
- Developing a national voice to advocate for holistic medicine
- Actively participating in the formation of legislation developing around the country that affects the practice of holistic medicine
- Increasing the number of physicians who are adequately trained and board certified in holistic medicine through the ABIHM

Organizations

The American Holistic Medical Association (AHMA) was founded in 1978 as a 501(c)(3) nonprofit membership organization for physicians seeking to practice a broader form of medicine than what was (and is) currently taught in allopathic and osteopathic (MD and DO) medical schools. For more than 30 years, the AHMA has nurtured and educated physicians making this transition.

The current membership includes approximately 800 doctors (including MDs, DOs, NDs, DCs, and others), medical students, residents, and licensed healthcare professionals (e.g., nurses, physician assistants, acupuncturists, nutritionists, massage therapists). A "Friend" membership category is open to CAM practitioners and others who are interested in supporting holistic health care.

AHMA is helping transform health care through collaboration, communication, education, and advocacy. www.holisticmedicine. org, 23366 Commerce Park, Suite 101B, Beachwood, Ohio 44122, PH (216) 292-6644, FAX (216) 292-6688.

Holistic Nursing

Carla Mariano, EdD, RN, AHN-BC, FAAIM

Partner Organization: American Holistic Nurses Association

About the Author: Carla Mariano developed and is former coordinator of the Adult Holistic Nurse Practitioner Program at New York University College of Nursing, and past president, American Holistic Nurses Association (AHNA).

Philosophy, Mission, and Goals

In 2006, holistic nursing was recognized by the American Nurses Association (ANA) as an official nursing specialty with a defined scope and standards of practice within the discipline of nursing. Holistic nursing emanates from five core values summarizing the ideals and principles of the specialty. These core values are:

- Philosophy, Theory, Ethics
- Holistic Caring Process
- Holistic Communication, Therapeutic Environment, and Cultural Diversity
- Holistic Education and Research
- Holistic Nurse Self-Care

Holistic nursing:
- Embraces all nursing which has enhancement of healing the whole person across the life-span and the health-illness continuum as its goal
- Recognizes the interrelationship of the unified bio-psychosocial-cultural-spiritual-energetic-environmental dimensions of the person
- Focuses on protecting, promoting, and optimizing health and wellness, assisting healing, preventing illness and injury,

alleviating suffering, and supporting people to find meaning, peace, comfort, harmony, and balance through the diagnosis and treatment of human response

- Views the nurse as an instrument of healing and a facilitator in the healing process
- Honors the individual's subjective experience about health, illness, health beliefs, and values
- Uses the caring-healing relationship and therapeutic partnership with individuals, families, and communities
- Draws on nursing knowledge, theories, research, expertise, intuition, and creativity
- Encourages peer review of professional practice in various clinical settings and integrates knowledge of current professional standards, laws, and regulations governing nursing practice
- Focuses on integrating self-reflection, self-care, and self-responsibility in personal/professional life
- Emphasizes awareness of the interconnectedness of self, others, nature, and God/Life/Spirit/Universal Force

Characteristics and Data

There are 2.9 million nurses in the US, of which 5,000–8,000 identify as holistic nurses and 4,150 are members of the American Holistic Nurses Association (AHNA)

Scope of Practice

- Draw on nursing knowledge, theories of wholeness, research and evidence-based practice, expertise, caring, and intuition to become therapeutic partners with clients and significant others in a mutually evolving process toward healing, balance, and wholeness
- Integrate holistic and alternative/complementary (CAM) modalities including, for example, relaxation, meditation, guided imagery, breath work, biofeedback, aroma and music therapies, touch therapies, acupressure, herbal remedies and natural supplements, homeopathy, reflexology, Reiki, journaling, exercise, stress management, nutrition, self-care processes, and prayer with conventional nursing interventions

- Conduct holistic assessments of physical, functional, psycho-social, emotional, mental, sexual, cultural, age-related, spiritual, beliefs/values/preferences, family issues, lifestyle patterns, environmental, and energy field status
- Select appropriate interventions in the context of the client's total needs and evaluate care in partnership with the client
- Assist clients to explore self-awareness, spirituality, growth, and personal transformation in healing
- Work to alleviate clients' signs and symptoms while empowering clients to access their own natural healing capacities
- Concentrate on the underlying meanings of symptoms and changes in the client's life patterns
- Provide comprehensive health counseling and education, health promotion, disease prevention, and risk reduction
- Guide clients/families between the conventional allopathic medical system and complementary/alternative therapies and systems
- Collaborate with and refer to other healthcare providers/ resources as necessary
- Advocate to provide access to and equitable distribution of healthcare resources, and to transform the healthcare system to a more caring culture
- Participate in building an ecosystem that sustains the well-being of the environment and the health of people, communities, and the planet
- Practice in numerous settings including ambulatory care, acute care, home care, private practitioner offices, wellness and complementary care centers, women's health centers, employee/student health, psychiatric mental health facilities, and schools
- Holistic nurses with advanced education can become advanced practice nurses, faculty, and researchers

Education

Nursing Programs in the US (ANA, 2007)
  113 Doctoral programs (PhD, EdD, DNS, DNP)
  438 Master's programs (MA, MS, MSN, MEd)
  694 Baccalaureate programs (BS, BSN)
  800 Associate programs (AD, ADN)

American Holistic Nurses Certification Corporation (AHNCC) Endorsed Academic Programs in Holistic Nursing
   3 Master's; 13 Baccalaureate

Nursing Accrediting Bodies
   American Association of Colleges of Nursing (AACN)
   National League for Nursing (NLN)

Certifying Organizations for Holistic Nursing
   American Holistic Nurses Certification Corporation (AHNCC)

Regulation and Certification

- National Licensure Exam (NCLEX) for all nurses through the National Council of State Boards of Nursing
- 25 (47%) State Boards of Nursing have a formal policy, position, or inclusion of holistic/complementary/alternative therapies in the scope of practice of nurses
- National Board Certification in Holistic Nursing at the basic (HN-BC) or advanced (AHN-BC) levels through the American Holistic Nurses Certification Corporation (AHNCC)
- Published *Scope and Standards of Holistic Nursing Practice (2007)* at the basic and advanced levels through the American Holistic Nurses Association (AHNA)

Research

Quantitative

   Outcome measures of various holistic therapies, e.g., therapeutic touch, prayer, relaxation, aromatherapy; instrument development to measure caring behaviors and dimensions; spirituality; self-transcendence; cultural competence; client responses to holistic interventions in health/illness

Qualitative

   Explorations of clients' lived experiences with various health/illness phenomena; theory development in healing, caring, intentionality, cultural constructions, empowerment, etc.

Challenges and Opportunities 2009–2015

Education
- Integration of holistic philosophy, content, and practices into nursing curricula nationally and staff development programs
- Recognition, support, and legitimization of holistic integrative nursing practice in accreditation, licensure, and credentialing processes

Research
- Identification and description of outcomes of holistic therapies such as healing, well-being, harmony
- Funding nurses for CAM and wholeness research
- Dissemination of nursing research findings to broader audiences including other health disciplines and public media

Practice
- Influence and change the healthcare system to a more humanistic orientation
- Development of caring cultures within healthcare delivery models and systems
- Collaboration with diverse healthcare disciplines to advance holistic health care
- Improvement of the nursing shortage through incorporation of self-care and stress-management practices for nurses and improvement of healthcare environments

Policy
- Reimbursement for holistic nursing practices and services
- Education of the public about the array of healthcare alternatives and providers
- Increase focus on wellness, health promotion, access, and affordability of health care to all populations
- Care of the environment

Organizations

American Holistic Nurses Association (AHNA) (founded 1982), Phone: 800-278-2462, Email: info@ahna.org; Website: www. ahna.org. AHNA , the definitive voice of holistic nursing, has been the leader in developing and advancing holistic philosophy, principles, standards, and guidelines for practice, education, and research. AHNA is committed to promoting wholeness and wellness in individuals, families, communities, nurses themselves, the nursing profession, and the environment. Through its various activities, AHNA integrates the art and science of nursing in the profession; unites nurses in healing; focuses on health, preventive education, and the integration of conventional and complementary caring healing modalities; honors individual excellence in the advancement of holistic nursing; and influences policy for positive change in the healthcare system.

American Nurses Association (ANA) http://www.nursing world.org/FunctionalMenu Categories/AboutANA/WhoWeAre. aspx. The ANA represents the interests of the nation's 2.9 million registered nurses (RNs) through its 51 constituent member associations, and its 24 specialty nursing and workforce advocacy organizations that currently connect to ANA as affiliates. The ANA advances the nursing profession by fostering high standards of nursing practice, promoting the rights of nurses in the workplace, projecting a positive and realistic view of nursing, and by lobbying Congress and regulatory agencies on healthcare issues affecting nurses and the public.

Homeopathy

Todd Rowe, MD, MD(H), CCH, DHt

Partner Organization: American Medical College of Homeopathy

About the Author: Todd Rowe, MD, MD(H), CCH, DHt is the founder and president of the American Medical College of Homeopathy. He is the president of the Arizona Board of Homeopathic and Integrated Medicine Examiners, has served on the board of directors for the Council for Homeopathic Certification and is a past president of the National Center for Homeopathy.

Philosophy, Mission, Goals

Homeopathic medicine is a form of alternative medicine that is holistic, scientifically based, safe to use, and inexpensive. Homeopathy can be effective in both acute and chronic disease and can be useful in many emergency situations as well. It is a system of medicine that is unique and distinct from other systems, disciplines, or modalities such as biomedicine, naturopathic medicine, herbal medicine, acupuncture, nutritional medicine, and mind-body medicine. Homeopathy uses minute doses of natural substances to activate the body's self-regulatory healing mechanisms. It was founded by Samuel Hahnemann over 200 years ago, although the principles on which it is based have been utilized in healing for thousands of years. Since its inception, homeopathy has been used by people from all walks of life, all ages, and in countries all over the world.

Characteristics and Data

Homeopathic medicine is the second most common form of alternative medicine in the world today and the most common in some higher income countries.[1] Homeopathic medicine was first introduced into the US in 1825 where it flourished until around 1900 when it began to meet opposition from conventional medicine. At that time, there were 22 homeopathic medical colleges and

20% of physicians used homeopathic medicine. The number of current homeopathic practitioners in this country is estimated at 8500.[2] There are four subgroups practicing homeopathy in some form in the Unites States. Standards, regulation, licensure, and educational accreditation vary widely among these groups.

- *Lay homeopaths:* No training standards, testing or recognition. Member organization is National Center for Homeopathy (NCH).
- *Professional homeopaths:* Not licensed as health care professionals; typically 850–900 hours training; Council on Homeopathic Certification tests; no external recognition, accreditation, or licensure; member organization is North American Society of Homeopaths (NASH). Health freedom legislation covers these practitioners in some states.
- *Registered homeopathic medical assistant:* 300 hours training required by state registration boards in AZ, NV; MD or DO supervision required.
- *Licensed health care professionals:* Training ranges from 200–300 hours to 1000 hours, depending on the field and the level of specialization.

Scope of Practice

The scope of practice varies considerably from state to state and is defined by various licensing agencies as well as, in some states, health freedom legislation. Homeopathic licensing boards exist in Arizona, Connecticut, and Nevada for MDs/DOs; in 15 states a section of ND board exams is on homeopathy.

Integration Activities

Homeopathic schools offer services in many off-site clinics. Examples of clinical areas of practice include fertility, acute care, incarcerated adolescents, low-income Hispanic population, substance abuse, homeless/free clinic, urgent care centers, and nursing homes. Homeopathic practitioners are sought out to provide expertise in the field of complementary medicine, including policy development, medical training, medical research, and clinical applications of natural therapies. Homeopaths Without Borders offers volunteer services to individuals living in regions facing crisis conditions. Combined degree programs are offered in Homeopathic Medicine and Acupuncture.

Education

Homeopathy has several levels of education standards reflecting requirements in the 4 subgroups of practitioners noted above, plus a given practitioner's level or specialization. There are currently 30 homeopathic schools in the US, 15 of which are listed in the school directory of the North American Network of Homeopathic Educators (NASH) and 3 of which are recognized by the Council for Homeopathic Education (CHE), the recognition body for homeopathic schools. Leaders of the CHE anticipate applying for recognition of CHE by the US Department of Education by March 2010. Naturopathic medicine is the only healthcare profession which requires homeopathic training based on Department of Education-recognized accrediting standards for all of its practitioners. Some conventional medical schools and residencies offer electives in homeopathic medicine.

Regulation and Certification

Laws regulating the practice of homeopathy vary from state to state. Usually it can be practiced legally by those whose license entitles them to practice a healthcare profession or medicine. (See scope of practice.) Health freedom laws in some states allow the practice of homeopathy by non-licensed professionals.

The Food and Drug Administration regulates the manufacture and sale of homeopathic medicines in the US. The Homeopathic Pharmacopoeia of the US was written into federal law in 1938 under the Federal Food, Drug, and Cosmetic Act, making the manufacture and sale of homeopathic medicines legal in this country (http://www.hpus.com). Since homeopathic remedies are sold over the counter, people in all states are free to use them for self-care at home.

Graduates of schools are eligible to test for national certification though various certifying organizations, the largest of which is the Council for Homeopathic Certification. The MD, DC, and ND professions each have specialty certification exams.

Research

The homeopathic profession has been conducting research for over 200 years. Several hundred studies have been published in recent years in clinical homeopathic research. A leading organization for homeopathic research is the Society for the Establishment of Research in Classical Homeopathy (SERCH). Homeopathic research focuses on five areas:

- Basic sciences research
- Clinical sciences research
- Educational research
- Homeopathic research
- Practice-based research

Challenges and Opportunities

Key challenges 2009–2012
- Increasing the public visibility of homeopathic medicine
- Expanding methods for legal practice
- Need for expansion of homeopathic research
- Opposition to regulation of the profession
- Need for improved educational standards for the profession

Key opportunities 2009–2012
- Potential for the development of bridge programs in homeopathic medicine for other healthcare professionals
- Increased demand for homeopathic services
- Growth and professionalization of homeopathic schools
- Active health freedom initiatives in multiple states
- Establishment of national homeopathic medical school

Organizations

The following are the principal national homeopathic organizations:
- Academy of Veterinary Homeopathy (AVH)
  www.theavh.org
- American Association of Homeopathic Pharmacists (AAHP)
  www.homeopathicpharmacy.org

- American Institute of Homeopathy (AIH)
  www.homeopathyusa.org
- Council for Homeopathic Certification (CHC)
  www.homeopathicdirectory.com
- Council on Homeopathic Education (CHE)
  www.chedu.org
- Homeopathic Academy of Naturopathic Physicians (HANP)
  www.hanp.net
- Homeopathic Nurses Association (HNA)
  www.nursehomeopaths.org
- Homeopathic Pharmacopoeia of the United States
  www.hpus.com/overview.php
- Homeopaths Without Borders (HWB)
  www.homeopathswithoutborders-na.org
- National Center for Homeopathy (NCH)
  www.nationalcenterforhomeopathy.org
- North American Network of Homeopathic Educators
  (NANHE)
  www.homeopathyeducation.org
- North American Society of Homeopaths (NASH)
  www.homeopathy.org

The National Center for Homeopathy is the national association for the profession. The North American Society of Homeopaths is the national association for homeopathic practitioners. The Council on Homeopathic Education is the national association for recognition of schools. The Council for Homeopathic Certification, Homeopathic Academy for Naturopathic Physicians, and the American Board of Homeotherapeutics are the main national certification bodies for homeopathic practitioners.

Citations

1. Ong CK, Bodeker G, Grundy C, Burford G, Shein K. *World Health Organization Global Atlas of Traditional Complementary and Alternative Medicine (Map Volume)*. Kobe, Japan; 2005.
2. National Homeopathic Practitioner Survey. http://www.amcofh.org/Research/CommunityScienceResearch.html. Accessed November 17, 2009.

Integrative Medicine

Victor S. Sierpina, MD

Partner Organization: Consortium of Academic Health Centers for Integrative Medicine

About the Author: Sierpina is the W.D. and Laura Nell Nicholson professor of integrative medicine and professor of family medicine at the University of Texas Medical Branch. He is the current chair of the Consortium of Academic Health Centers for Integrative Medicine.

Note: Integrative medicine is a movement to transform medicine led by a growing set of leaders from conventional academic health centers. The lead agency in that movement is the Consortium of Academic Health Centers for Integrative Medicine.

The Consortium of Academic Health Centers for Integrative Medicine is composed of 42 North American academic health science centers (as of April 2009) that have active programs in at least two of the three areas of education, clinical care, and research in integrative medicine and have support at the Dean's level or above. The Consortium defines Integrative Medicine as "...the practice of medicine that reaffirms the importance of the relationship between practitioner and patient, focuses on the whole person, is informed by evidence, and makes use of all appropriate therapeutic approaches, healthcare professionals and disciplines to achieve optimal health and healing."

The Consortium started with eight schools in 1999 and, with the generous support of the Bravewell Philanthropic Collaborative for infrastructure, has grown rapidly, expanding to 23 schools by 2003, 36 in 2006, and 45 in 2009. For a complete list of member schools and other Consortium information, see the website at www.imconsortium.org.

The mission of the Consortium is "to advance the principles and practices of integrative healthcare within academic institutions." The Consortium provides its institutional membership with a community of support for their academic missions and a collective voice for influencing change. The goals of the Consortium are as follows:

- Stimulate changes in medical education that facilitate the adoption of integrative medicine curricula
- Develop and promote policies and practices that enhance access to integrative models of care
- Undertake collaborative projects to promote and conduct research and disseminate the findings
- Inform national policy that advances integrative medicine through research, clinical, and education initiatives

With the voice of over 30% of US and almost 25% of Canadian medical schools, the Consortium is poised to continue to advocate within academia for a relevant role for integrative medicine, across all institutional missions. By collaborating with such organizations as ACCAHC, the Consortium hopes to make a broad impact across all disciplines in integrative models of education, practice, and research. The Consortium invited ACCAHC to assist in planning a large international research conference in 2009. The Consortium and ACCAHC also held at that same conference a joint leadership meeting to plan and develop formal inter-organizational activities and projects.

Leadership and Working Groups

The Consortium leadership is composed of a Steering Committee member from each of the 45 schools. An Executive Committee is comprised of Chair, Vice-Chair, Treasurer, Secretary, and the immediate past Chair and Vice-Chair, as well as six at-large members. It is governed by by-laws and is an IRS-recognized nonprofit 501(c)(3) organization.

The Consortium operationalizes many of its efforts through its working groups. Through monthly phone calls, group members identify areas of shared interest and significant impact.

Education Working Group

The Education Working Group is continuously involved in fostering projects in integrative medical education. Previous projects have included creating a curriculum guide containing exemplars of integrative medicine teaching that were shared with all medical school education deans, co-authoring an article on proposed competencies for a medical school curriculum in integrative medicine, coordinating a grant from the Bravewell Collaborative to foster mind-body training and curriculum among the Consortium schools, and creating a presentation about the Consortium for deans at three regional Generalists in Medical Education Conferences of the Association of American Medical Colleges.

Other efforts have included proposing a change in educational standards to the Licensing Commission for Medical Education (LCME), authoring test questions on integrative medicine for licensing and certification board exams, and compiling a database of educational resources in CAM/IM education available in the US and Canada for other centers wishing to access such materials for their own ongoing or nascent programs. The Education Working Group also submits publications such as letters to the editor, responses to editorials and opinion pieces, as well as ad hoc white papers. A student leadership committee helps foster leadership training at the American Medical Student Association.

Clinical Working Group

The Clinical Working Group examines clinical initiatives across the member schools and shares expertise, clinical models, and business issues, as well as fostering clinical research. Several schools have IRB approval to participate in The Outcomes Research Project to examine patient outcomes related to integrative medicine. In addition to the core working group, the Clinical Working Group has created collaborations with three subgroups, Integrative Oncology, Pediatrics, and Integrative Mental Health. The Clinical Working Group has also developed a Clinical Models Survey, which is an audit of clinical services of Consortium members. They are also developing the infrastructure for a practice-based research network in collaboration with the Research Working Group. The Clinical Working Group also has a goal to define key components that constitute an integrative medicine clinic, such as process issues, philosophy, and function. This will help improve the function of existing integrative medicine clinics and will also help in developing new clinic sites.

Research Working Group

The Research Working Group has created a network of researchers from the various schools to share their expertise and patient populations for recruitment in studies in integrative medicine. By developing this membership database with information about research, practice, areas of expertise, and ongoing projects, the Research Working Group will foster collaboration and mentoring among members. This information will also be used to establish a Rapid Response and Referral Network for fielding questions from the media and providing comment on complementary and alternative medicine (CAM) and integrative medicine related topics. The Research Working Group is instrumental for the Consortium's Complementary and Integrative Medicine Research Conference, for which members serve as contributors and scientific reviewers.

Policy

Another vital activity of the Consortium is the policy domain, where our stated goal is to "… inform national policy that advances integrative medicine through research, clinical, and education initiatives."

The Consortium has crafted attractive, informative "leave behinds" describing the Consortium and integrative medicine; they are appropriate for beginning dialogue with legislators, policy makers, and other opinion leaders. We developed a process and policy for establishing collaborations and networking with other organizations in the CAM community. Policy initiatives also include meetings with the leadership of the National Center for Complementary and Alternative Medicine of the National Institutes of Health, the Institute of Medicine, and with campus government relations officers in member schools.

Challenges and Opportunities

While the future of integrative medicine education is bright, some major challenges and opportunities lie ahead for us to prepare the next generation of integrative medicine practitioners. Among these are:

- Faculty development in both conventional and CAM schools regarding the content of the field, teaching methods, and research expertise
- Transprofessional collaboration in education, research, clinical care, and healthcare policy among integrative medicine practitioners and colleagues in conventional medicine, allied

health, nursing, pharmacy, and CAM disciplines such as chiropractic, massage, naturopathic medicine, indigenous healthcare systems, and others

- Providing learners with critical thinking skills, access to reliable resources, and role modeling of integrative practice in consistent, credible, and relevant ways
- Outcomes-based practice and optimal care pathways informed by research
- Changes in health insurance reimbursement and policy to provide broader access to integrative medicine for underserved patients

To advance such an agenda, the Consortium must partner with other CAM organizations and professional educators, deans and course directors in our medical, nursing, and allied health schools, researchers, health policy and opinion leaders, patient advocacy groups, and the scientific community. Together, we can change the world of health care.

Resources

- Consortium website: www.imconsortium.org.
- Research conference: North American Research Conferences on Complementary and Integrative Medicine (May 2006, May 2009, May 2012): www.imconsortium-conference.org/
- Consortium-endorsed: Core competencies in integrative medicine for medical school curricula: a proposal. *Acad Med.* 2004;79:521-531.
- Featured articles: *Academic Medicine* issue with 10 articles on CAM educational programs in medical and nursing schools, with major involvement by multiple Consortium programs. *Acad Med.* 2007;82.

Yoga Therapy

John Kepner, MA, MBA

Partner Organization: International Association of Yoga Therapists

About the Author: Kepner is the executive director of the International Association of Yoga Therapists.

Philosophy, Mission, and Goals

Due to the long history and diverse nature of the yoga tradition, there is not a consensus definition of the field. As defined by IAYT, however, "Yoga therapy is the process of empowering individuals to progress towards improved health and well-being through the application of the philosophy and practice of Yoga." The most widely embraced guide to the philosophy of yoga is the Yoga Sutras of Patanjali and the most common practices are postures (*asanas*), breath control (*pranayama*), deep relaxation, and meditation.

The distinction between yoga and yoga therapy is not clear cut and depends, in part, upon the language used by different yoga methods and the context. In general, however, yoga therapy is an orientation to the practice of yoga that is focused on healing, as opposed to fitness, wellness, or spiritual support. It is often taught privately, as well as in group classes.

Characteristics and Data

The actual number of practicing yoga teachers and therapists cannot be accurately assessed. The field is unregulated and individuals are free to describe themselves as yoga teachers or therapists. In a survey taken in 2003, the *Yoga Journal* estimated that there were over 100,000 yoga teachers in the US alone.

Scope of Practice

The scope of practice varies by method and philosophy, but most commonly can be described as the management of structural aches and pains, chronic disease, emotional imbalance, stress, and spiritual challenges using the student's own body, breath, and mind.

Integration Activities

IAYT nurtures affiliations with the Yoga Alliance (YA) and the National Ayurvedic Medical Association (NAMA). Other collaborations include meeting/symposia, educational sponsorships, bridge-building dialogues, organizational affiliations with ACCAHC, and participating in the North American Research Conference on Complementary and Integrative Medicine.

Education

The training of yoga therapists is generally provided by private schools and/or supported by traditional yoga lineages. The 47 member schools of IAYT (as of 2009) likely provide the overwhelming majority of the training and certification of yoga therapists, at least in the US. The content and length of therapist training varies widely, with most programs clustering around 500 hours (including basic teacher training), or 1,000 hours plus. In 2009, IAYT and its member schools formally launched a two-year effort to develop recommended standards for the training of Yoga therapists.

Yoga teachers and yoga therapists do not have accredited schools, and yoga courses are rarely included in curricula of degreed institutes of higher learning. This is slowly changing, however, and some yoga and yoga therapy certification courses are beginning to be taught at universities.

Regulation and Certification

Yoga therapy is an unregulated discipline. In the US, the profession is broadly represented by the International Association of Yoga Therapists (IAYT). IAYT is currently spearheading an effort to develop voluntary training standards for yoga therapists. IAYT maintains a public directory of members, many of whom provide a professional profile describing their education, training and experience.

There is no certifying or regulating body for yoga teaching professionals. Yoga Alliance (YA), a non-profit organization, has a voluntary registry of yoga teachers (RYTs) and schools (RYSs) who meet widely accepted standards of training and education.

Certification as a yoga teacher or yoga therapist is generally provided by individual schools or lineage associations. The training of yoga therapists varies widely, hence the efforts of IAYT and member schools to develop standards.

Research

The National Institutes of Health support basic research into yoga. Yoga is classified as mind-body medicine by the National Center for Complementary and Alternative Medicine.

IAYT is actively involved with promoting research in the field of yoga therapy. Its peer-reviewed journal, the *International Journal of Yoga Therapy* (IJYT), and its annual professional meeting, the Symposium for Yoga Therapy and Research (SYTAR) www.sytar.org, are the two major association forums to promote and support research in yoga therapy.

Challenges and Opportunities

Key challenges 2009–2012
- Developing a consensus definition of the field
- Developing training standards that are credible to both the yoga community and the healthcare community and that also recognize the diversity inherent in the field
- Supporting the professional credibility of the field through research, education, and professional meetings
- Sustaining the practice as a healing discipline, given the legal legacy of restricting health care to licensed professions
- Helping the public find a qualified practitioner for particular needs and interests

Key opportunities 2009–2012
The practice of yoga is a low-cost, effective method for promoting wellness and supporting healing at many levels. A key element

for yoga is that, once trained, individuals can practice without professional supervision.

The practice has grown tremendously over the past ten years, in part because the practice is so adaptable to the young and the old, the fit and the not-so-fit, the exercise enthusiast and the spiritual seeker. It is an especially suitable wellness practice for an aging population.

Given the growth and popularity of the field in the West in the past 10 years, the emerging research supporting its many healing properties, the growing acceptance of complementary and alternative therapies in general, and the high cost of conventional care, there are many opportunities to develop the field as a stand-alone healing practice or in conjunction with conventional and CAM healthcare fields.

Since yoga is not a licensed practice, the practice is not constrained by insurance reimbursement practices.

Organizations and Websites

The International Association of Yoga Therapists (IAYT) is a nonprofit 501(c)(3) professional association. IAYT supports research and education in yoga and serves as a professional organization for yoga teachers and yoga therapists worldwide. Our mission is to establish yoga as a recognized and respected therapy and our website is www.iayt.org. IAYT publishes the *International Journal of Yoga Therapy,* a peer-reviewed journal, *Yoga Therapy Today,* and the IAYT Digital Resources Library http://iayt.fmdrl.org. IAYT provides a search function for the public to find members in their area and sponsors an annual Symposium on Yoga Therapy and Research (SYTAR). As of 2009, IAYT has approximately 2,600 individual members and 46 school members.

Yoga Alliance is a nonprofit organization supported by over 25,000 yoga teachers and schools. Yoga Alliance registered teachers and schools are recognized for meeting internationally recognized standards of training, experience, and ongoing professional development. Protecting the health and safety of society, these standards encompass the many aspects of yoga including anatomy and physiology, yoga philosophy, yoga lifestyle and ethics, teaching methodology, and techniques training, providing teachers with an important foundation for their yoga teaching practice. Acknowledged by the designations RYT, E-RYT, and RYS, Yoga Alliance Registered Yoga Teachers (RYT) and Registered Yoga Schools (RYS) can be found at www.yogaalliance.org.